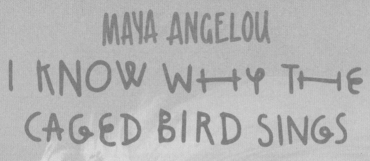

MAYA ANGELOU
I KNOW WHY THE CAGED BIRD SINGS

INTRODUCED BY TAYARI JONES
ILLUSTRATED BY SHABAZZ LARKIN

GRANTA

12 Addison Avenue, London W11 4QR | email: editorial@granta.com
To subscribe go to granta.com, or call 020 8955 7011 in the United Kingdom,
845-267-3031 (toll-free 866-438-6150) in the United States

ISSUE 154: WINTER 2021

p.134 extract from 'Ask' by Cheran from *In a Time of Burning*, reproduced by permission of Arc Publications; p.140 extract from 'Small passing' by Ingrid de Kok from *Seasonal Fires: New and Selected Poems*, reproduced by permission of Seven Stories Press; p.144 Solmaz Sharif, excerpt from 'Personal Effects' from *Look*. Copyright © 2016 by Solmaz Sharif. Reprinted with the permission of The Permissions Company, LLC on behalf of Graywolf Press, graywolfpress.org; p.145–46 extracts from 'Nanabhai Bhatt in Prison' by Sujata Bhatt from *Collected Poems*, reproduced by kind permission of Carcanet Press Ltd, Manchester; p.150–51 extracts from 'July 1983' by Anne Ranasinghe from *Against Eternity and Darkness*, reproduced by permission of Shanti Conly on behalf of the Ranasinghe family.

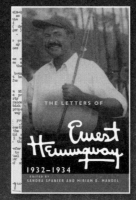

Romanticism
100 POEMS

EDITED BY MICHAEL FERBER

ISBN: 9781108491051

THE LETTERS OF

Ernest Hemingway

1932–1934

SANDRA SPANIER AND MIRIAM B. MANDEL

ISBN: 9780521897372

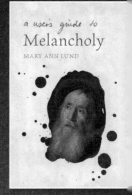

a user's guide to
Melancholy
MARY ANN LUND

ISBN: 9781108838849

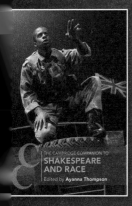

THE CAMBRIDGE COMPANION TO
SHAKESPEARE AND RACE
Edited by **Ayanna Thompson**

ISBN: 9781108710565

THE CAMBRIDGE COMPANION TO
THEATRE AND SCIENCE
Edited by **Kirsten E. Shepherd-Barr**

ISBN: 9781108700986

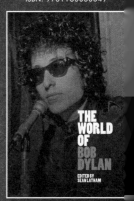

THE WORLD OF **BOB DYLAN**
EDITED BY SEAN LATHAM

ISBN: 9781108499514

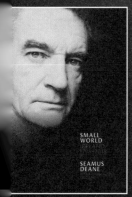

SMALL WORLD

SEAMUS DEANE

ISBN: 9781108840866

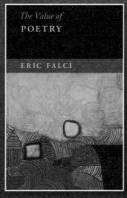

The Value of
POETRY

ERIC FALCI

ISBN: 9781108454476

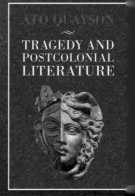

ATO QUAYSON
TRAGEDY AND POSTCOLONIAL LITERATURE

ISBN: 9781108830980

ambridge.org/granta21

OLLOW US ON SOCIAL MEDIA:
CUP_LitPerform CUPLiteraturePerformance

CAMBRIDGE
UNIVERSITY PRESS

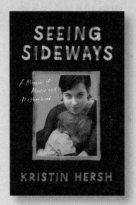

A follow-up to the critically acclaimed *Rat Girl*, this beautifully written memoir takes readers on an emotional journey through the author's life as she reflects on thirty years of music and motherhood.

Seeing Sideways

A Memoir of Music and Motherhood

BY KRISTIN HERSH

$27.95 hardcover | May 2021

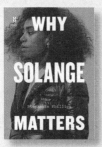

Why Solange Matters

BY STEPHANIE PHILLIPS

A Black feminist punk performer and important new voice recounts the dramatic story of an incandescent musician and artist whose unconventional journey to international success on her own terms was far more important than her family name.

$18.95 paperback | April 2021

Why Marianne Faithfull Matters

BY TANYA PEARSON

A remarkable feminist history and biography that features fragments from the five-decade career of an iconic artist, who, despite a private life that overshadowed much of her early work, sculpted her own musical rebirth.

$18.95 paperback | July 2021

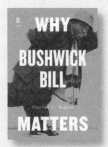

Why Bushwick Bill Matters

BY CHARLES HUGHES

An astute chronicle of the life and cultural significance of Bushwick Bill, who remixed spectacle as he exposed and exploited ableist and racist assumptions to become a singular voice in rap and the relentless battle over free speech in the United States.

$18.95 paperback | June 2021

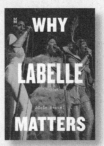

Why Labelle Matters

BY ADELE BERTEI

Crafting a legacy all their own, the reinvented Labelle subverted the "girl group" aesthetic to invoke the act's Afrofuturist spirit and make manifest their vision of Black womanhood.

$18.95 paperback | March 2021

The Courtauld

Our vibrant new programme of Short Courses in Art History for 2021

t: +44 (0)20 39477 650
e: short.courses@courtauld.ac.uk
web: courtauld.ac.uk/learn

Granta readers **Save 40%**
on Subscriptions + Free tote bag

———

12 Months for **£20.95** (+p&p)

Aesthetica

aestheticamagazine.com/shop

Image Credit: Diane Villadsen. Model: Miki Hamano. Location: San Francisco (2017). Courtesy of the artist.

£16.99
(plus p&p)

Less time searching, more time writing

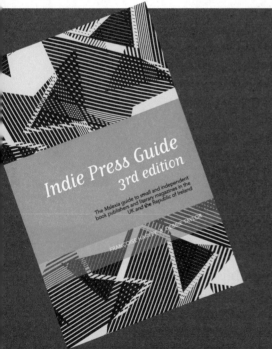

The *Indie Press Guide* provides details of over 600 literary magazines and presses. It's a must have staple for any writer and is loved and trusted by thousands of authors across the UK and the Republic of Ireland. All entries are classified by genre, with practical publication details such as:

❭ how to submit
❭ fees and prices
❭ production standards
❭ contact details

You won't find this valuable information collected together anywhere else! Now it's over to you...

'I'VE BEEN OFFERED PUBLICATION BY AN INDIE PRESS WHICH I'VE ACCEPTED. IT WAS ALL BECAUSE OF YOUR PUBLICATION.'
HELEN YOUNG

www.mslexia.co.uk
postbag@mslexia.co.uk
0191 204 8860

mslexia

CONTENTS

Introduction

The cover of this issue is a painting by Tom Hammick. The title is *Vergissmeinnicht*, German for forget-me-not, the small blue flower. Tom told me that he took the title from a poem by Keith Douglas, written during the North Africa campaign of World War II. Douglas and his group discover a dead German soldier in the desert, on recaptured land – 'Three weeks gone and the combatants gone / returning over the nightmare ground'. It's only when they find a photograph in the gun pit, signed 'Steffi. Vergissmeinnicht', that Douglas begins to think of the dead soldier as anything other than simply an enemy. Steffi would weep, he thinks, at the sight of the flies on the dead man's face; 'the dust upon the paper eye / and the burst stomach like a cave'.

Within a year or so Douglas himself was dead, killed in Normandy, aged twenty-four.

Vergissmeinnicht. 55,000 dead and counting, in the UK, as I write. By the time you read this, many more people will have died, but for most of us, what we think of as 'normal life' may have resumed – a vaccine; Trump resigned to defeat; a Brexit deal concluded. Some of us, I notice, carry on almost as normal, but aren't we all a bit frayed around the edges, worn out by – what exactly, if we are not ill? The proximity to illness? Lockdown restrictions? Isolation? The news? I don't know. The title of this issue – taken from Dan Shurley's story – reflects fatigue, and perhaps sadness. But, in defiance of sadness, we are introducing a vibrant new voice: Catalan poet Eva Baltasar, with 'Permafrost', an extract from her forthcoming novel.

Lindsey Hilsum remembers reporting from Goma, a small border town in what was then Zaire, now the Democratic Republic of the Congo, among hundreds of thousands of Hutu refugees from Rwanda. By April 1994 the genocide was over, and some two million Hutus, many of them killers or collaborators, were fleeing the country. International media and aid organisations descended on this small town on the edge of a volcano, mingling with refugees who, within days, started succumbing to a cholera epidemic. There was no clean water, and at times no water at all. Journalists staying in colonial villas stepped cautiously around bodies, instructed not to bring abandoned children to the aid tents, because all hope of reuniting them with their parents would then be lost. Many of those children must have died. Mothers and fathers, who may have taken part in genocide, lay dying on the side of the road. Hilsum, who had reported from Rwanda during the genocide, knew the history well, but what do you do with the knowledge that the victims of today are yesterday's perpetrators?

P oet Vidyan Ravinthiran meditates on similarly ambiguous themes in his autobiographical essay, 'Victim and Accused'. He visits a group of mothers in Sri Lanka whose children – mostly young men, but women too – went missing in the civil war. The government has promised records, but none have been produced. The mothers are in limbo; their children are probably, but not certainly, dead. Ravinthiran is in his own, less desperate, limbo. He has lost his precarious sense of belonging in Brexit Britain; lost his poetic voice onstage and his confidence in teaching. Progressive white people sometimes fear saying the wrong thing when the issue is race and their interlocutor is not white; this silence, or fragility, contributes to Ravinthiran's sense of alienation. He also touches, in his essay, on the thorny issue of comparative suffering. There can be no comparison, obviously, between his own suffering and the suffering of the mothers in Sri Lanka. 'But,' he writes, 'I'm curious about the refusal to countenance a connection between disparate experiences – a route by which empathy could travel.'

We have now conducted two Zoom launches, for the summer and autumn issues of *Granta*. I have been moved – this sounds trivial, but bear with me – by seeing the chat bar on the side fill up with warm and respectful comments as people listened to contributors reading: that too, it seems to me, is a route by which empathy travels. Perhaps in isolation a new form of communication is emerging, expressing what readers and writers have always told one another, via books and letters and on the literary stage: I hear you. You are not alone. ∎

Sigrid Rausing

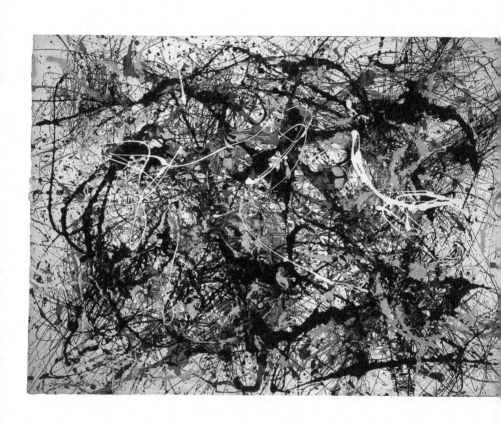

PERMAFROST

Eva Baltasar

TRANSLATED FROM THE CATALAN BY JULIA SANCHES

She was French. Marseillaise, actually, like the national anthem. The nerve center of her beauty resided in her being French. I was in love with her nationality, a second face with perfect features cast over the first like a semitransparent film, but with the charm of the great classics. Her name was Roxanne and she was shorter than me, slimmer than me, more intelligent and nobler than me. She was more educated, too: a PhD in literature with diplomas in English, German and Italian. On top of all of that, she was magnificent on the piano. She had one at home in a large room that I pompously referred to as the piano room and where she played long pieces from memory. She was, as Mom would put it, from a good family, and this being-from-a-good-family showed on her like a coat of varnish. In fact, it showed in every single gesture, no matter how insignificant. For example, she had a particular way of moving her chin when opening the door, lifting it very slightly to one side while casting her eyes down, and I always felt like she took for granted that someone would step aside for her. It's hard to explain – but it was obvious when I saw it. She was a climber and though at the time I couldn't imagine my life without her, the moment I saw her naked body, I decided all my future lovers should have loved climbing in their past. Her muscles were perfect, thrumming and covered in supple, impeccable skin. Her every position in bed was an anatomical study in red chalk – improbably precise and as exciting as a first visit to Casa Buonarroti. I remember her stomach – quiet and commanding like a tortoise shell – and the tensed arch of her arms, her ass, her thighs and her calves – compact like thinking skulls – all centered on me and my pleasure alone, on reaching the summit of my pleasure. Never before nor since have I spent so many nights screwing. By that I mean whole nights, five or six or seven hours of relentless fucking, mostly with her on top. 'Talk to me in French,' I would ask. And she'd say some things I understood and others I didn't have to understand. It was enough just to listen to her, to let her words penetrate my body, softening it in strange and unpredictable ways. Her voice shook me violently, consumed me, a wisp of hair singed by a cigarette ember. My body shrank and coiled at once, assaulted by her accent like a doughy maggot being pricked by a pin. As I write this, I relive it, and millions of my cells pass along buckets of glowing water to put out goodness knows what fire. Fast and blind. My heart flares up, damaging the pleural membrane, which is so unaccustomed to playing along. Roxanne. When I met her, she'd just bought a professional camera. I envied the camera for spending all day in her hands, white with slender knuckles and polished tips. Before playing the piano, she used to splay her fingers over the keys, and it was as if they were simply resting for a moment, both contained and laid out, like a row of matching surgical tools before a very delicate intervention. Then she would subtly flex them and move them according to instructions from a series of neck muscles triggered milliseconds before her fingers. I listened as the sound of the piano strings penetrated me like her words, shaking me and giving rise to inexplicable surges and a sort of self-indulgent jealousy. I followed the unintelligible movement of her fingers as they drove the composition toward the moment when it would finally die out. She adored Satie. 'It's easy,' she said. And over and over she played 'Je te veux', the first 'Gymnopédie', and the second 'Nocturne'. 'They're so long,' I'd grumble. And she would laugh and retort, 'They're only three minutes,' then play them again. And I renewed myself in that image, of my French piano-playing lover. But every second I died. And it was a very dignified, respectable way to go.

'So, what's it like with a woman? In bed, I mean.'
    It's half past twelve and it's taken my sister two whole servings of almond chicken and fried rice to let her hair down. Or maybe it was the Coke. She hasn't had any in more than three years. Slow-acting poison, she calls it. But tonight is special. Not everybody has a lesbian sister to comfort them after a breakup. Tonight's heart-to-heart will be a real treat – irresistibly modern, maybe even obscene. My sister can't help picturing herself as the lead in a popular TV series. Playing the sister of the lesbian is quite the role; it offers a seal of respectability. 'Do you want Nestea?' I ask her before dinner. She throws me a thunderous look, as if she'd just decided to go into business with the Mafia. 'Screw it, I'll have the Coke!' she says, thrilled. Screw it! 'Careful it doesn't go to your head. You're not used to such strong beverages.' My sister doesn't know her way around a can, so I transfer the Coke into a tall glass that she takes from my hands with a wanton gleam in her eye. The poor thing feels funny, she's used to getting her beauty sleep. But great things are afoot! 'What's it like' – enticing inquiry – 'to fuck a woman?' I swear this is the first time she's ever uttered the word 'fuck', plumb-drunk on Coca-Cola. 'So that's what you wanted to know?' I ask with a dash of cruelty. I flat out refuse to suffer fools, even when they try to make an effort. 'You know that's not true!' she cries. I concentrate on the guest room and nothing but the guest room, crucial as fingernails. 'Shall I tell you another story?' She nods with a headful of eyes and the aspartame-laced smiles of a pampered girl who will never, never ever indulge in another can of Coke. 'All right,' I consent. The tactic works. 'Have you ever heard of action painting?' Now she shakes her head. 'Jackson Pollock?' I insist. 'No.' 'Okay.' I walk into my room and bring out a book of Pollock paintings. It's tremendous; images like these make me re-evaluate my love affair with death. 'This is art? A child could have made these!' my sister blurts. 'But a child didn't.' The woman must be dumb. Thick

as two planks. This guest room is costing me a tidy sum, but what else can I do? Where else can I go? The sweet-and-sour prawns are affecting my ability to think, but I have another go. I'm sure that with some effort I can pluck a plastic flower from the dunghill, a plastic flower that will satisfy the dregs of curiosity of the poor aborted lesbian lurking in my sister's brain. 'This is an action painting,' I begin. 'Action painting is the product of impatience.' She pulls a face like a cricket. 'Around the mid-twentieth century, there was a period when artists were no longer being challenged. For centuries, they'd struggled with a series of problems: motif, depth, form, color, realism, fidelity, light . . . everything! In other words, they'd run out of lines of inquiry. And then Pollock rocked up with his huge, unplanned canvases stretched out on the floor, and wham!' 'Wham?' 'Look at this.' I show her *Number 3*, flip pages, *Number 5*, flip pages, *Number 34*, a superb piece with that horrific red-thinking head and its two yellow hemispheres. 'Look,' I tell her. 'Clear, simple manipulation of raw material! Pure experimentation! Pollock splattered canvases driven by the spontaneity of the moment. A work of art isn't only the end result – it's art in time, art in real time, in action, as simple and impulsive as a drawing by a child. But there's a sophisticated concern below the surface, an interest in process – life's immensity concentrated in that process. Do you get what I'm saying?' 'Sort of.' 'All right. So now you sort of know what it's like to fuck a woman.'

Seven months had passed. Enough for it to have metastasized? I had no idea. The mole's growth had slowed. The bottom edge of its beautiful contour had blotted. Once a deep black, it was now a faded brown, consummated in a series of tiny specks that no longer formed part of the raised cluster but existed as solitary, pigmented entities hovering a few millimeters below what could still be considered the mole. To be safe, I canceled my appointment with the dermatologist and started the process from scratch. Ahead of me lay ten more months of waiting, ten months for the altered cells to migrate – not downward, but deep inside.

I always suspected that Roxanne was more suicidal than I was.
That she would die first, I had no doubt, but most of all, that her
desire for death had hardened within her into a formative whole. I
was also convinced that she would die a more elegant death. Someone
inside her was burnishing every single thing she did, every measured
word she said – but who? Catalan phrases strutted out of her throat
wrapped in French-accented mink, but with a lowly, port-like
fragrance that I attributed to her Marseilles roots and which drove
me wild. In her mouth, Catalan sounded the way it should sound as a
perfect language. Any word that I said immediately afterward was
a faded daisy in comparison, a silly little flower. I've never spoken
as sparingly as I did with her, and I've never enjoyed the lead-in to
a conversation quite as much. Whenever she opened her lips with a
click of the tongue that recalled a book whose pages lay open under
a strong wind, my heart would turn so slick it became an organ out
of control. Every beat, every deliberate whiplash of life was trapped
inside it. And it wasn't just my chest, either. Every part of me flared
up under the influence of her words. '*Què vols sopar*?' she'd ask. And
she would say it just like that, in italics, because she had the ability to
apply font to speech. She did it every time, and without realizing. It
made me dizzy. '*Encara queda Camembert del que vaig portar ahir*?'
And I was reduced to aftershocks of pleasure, at whose epicenter was
the word 'Camembert'. I tried my best to say something, stressing
the paroxytones in an effort to appear interesting. 'Of course. I had
salmon for lunch so we could have the Camembert for dinner.' Lies.
Big. Fat. Lies. I'd had sausage and beans, except I couldn't be with
Roxanne and also be someone who ate sausage and beans. Absolutely
not. I would have sausage for lunch, air out the apartment, take the
trash down to the dumpster, and claim I had salmon. Because even
though salmon isn't Camembert, it belongs to the same part of the
pyramid as the foods I used to save for days when I wanted to treat
myself, as Mom likes to put it, before I met Roxanne. This never made
sense to Roxanne, whose whole life was a treat. Roxanne often had
croissants for breakfast – flaky on the outside, insides soft, buttery,

and still warm. She bought them from a bakery four blocks from her house, where they were held for her. She drank coffee like I did, but not just any old coffee. She had her coffee delivered from a shop where it was ground *sur place* seconds before being packaged. She didn't have ordinary ham; she had smoked ham. When we ate at her place, she would cook a peculiar type of pasta that looked like a ruddy, serrated snail shell, sautéed with hot spices and served with sprout salad. She loved funky cheeses. She filled my fridge with Comté, Brie, Époisses de Bourgogne, Gaperon and Roquefort, none of which were labeled the way they usually were in supermarkets, if they stocked them in the first place. She got a different brand every time, each more authentic than the last, and imported. The same could be said of everything about her – her clothes, her hobbies, the building she lived in, her hair. She wore a single piece of jewelry: a striated ring the width of one finger on the middle finger of her right hand. She almost always dressed in dark clothes. She had pale skin and liked to wear baggy sweaters with long sleeves that fell halfway down her hand. I used to dream about those sweaters. I would dream of her white, silver-ringed hand as it emerged from a deep-blue sleeve, cold and slow like a sea mollusk. My eyes would fixate on her hand as it stirred pasta in the wok with the chopsticks she usually used to cook. I was captivated by that finger, her ring finger. It was perhaps her only concession to traditional constructs of femininity. Even though everything about her screamed femininity: head blonde and shorn like a solid and recently shaven cunt, cracked-ice eyes, breasts long and continuous like tongues resting over a flight of ribs, crimped nipples, legs and feet soft and monochrome like the drawings in the classical *Kama Sutra*. Her flesh was taut, smooth and moderately full, her mouth wild like a natural cleft in a chunk of mineral rock, and her tongue . . . her tongue was a sovereign being that lived alongside her, a slave to my pleasure. It talked to me and fucked me and carried on talking while Roxanne fucked me instead, a partially domesticated animal, dogged and feral when entering my cunt. She hadn't wanted to at first. 'I love it when you eat me out,' she said on our first night together, 'though I don't usually do it myself.' 'You'd better start.' Pleasure is a lower value, but Max Scheler had a knack for changing sides and change can be an excellent source of knowledge. She did it. It became her favorite part, in fact. She could keep at it all evening, like a lioness fixated on a wound. A slow, rhythmical licking. And I struck back. Our cunts were our favorite set of fine china. We plated them with fruit salad – segments of mandarin and sweet orange, which we peeled and sliced into pieces. We held fruit in our lips and between our teeth, dipped the pieces inside ourselves and fed them to one another. Now and then we doused each other in chocolate syrup or raspberry sauce, and if we spotted a seed, we would tuck it into the folds of our lips or lick it into the hole. Wiping myself after peeing the next day, I might come across a seed and smile. Innocent little seed, in a pee stain, on a piece of toilet paper. A childlike gemstone of immeasurable worth.

S he was a woman. By that, I mean a female rather than a male dermatologist. She wasn't attractive and yet the morning sun poured through the tall windows behind her with such force it seemed almost to penetrate her, magnifying her humanity and dressing her in a beauty that she certainly lacked outside the office. She'd just set beside her computer a small plastic cup rimmed with residues of coffee foam, and it occurred to me that her tongue must also be the intoxicated yellow that comes from drinking coffee. I was her first patient of the day. I'd arrived a little before eight and sat alone in the waiting room, rereading Kierkegaard and collecting myself. The doctor saw me right away. She was younger than me. Her white coat looked new and hung loose on her body. Next to the sink sat a small plant with a couple of buds about to bloom. That same morning, probably. She smiled at me and everything – her youth, her baggy coat, the plant, her smile – made me feel guilty. Did I really have to go and ruin this doctor's day? She seemed nice. What if this was her first case of melanoma diagnosed at a first consultation and during a first examination in a woman as young as I was? My mole was now more a meteor than a mole, a dark comet with a powerful trail of particles glowing behind it. Its suckerfish had multiplied in such a way that the entire mole seemed to have shifted, creeping a few centimeters up my stomach. According to my mother's calculations, no less than a couple of colonies of malignant cells should have already taken root in some shimmering organ inside me. I wasn't concerned about the fact that I had no symptoms. I was sure they'd show before long, just as soon as I had a confirmed diagnosis. I prayed for it to be too late to get treatment; I preferred a sudden growth and a predictable end. 'So, what can I help you with?' she asked, looking me square in the eyes. Hers were brown and they sparkled, as though her skull was a pumpkin and inside the flame of a candle was flickering. How could I get her to understand that I was beyond help? Without hurting her? Without snuffing out that lovely, animate, impermanent flame? In this woman? In vocation incarnate? In her white coat and *Sistine Madonna*-esque halo that the sharp light had drawn around her, filtered through the blinds? Did I really have to go and do that to her? On a morning bright enough to make buds bloom? Not me – I wasn't going to be the one to make her cry. 'My doctor told me I should have some moles checked out,' I said innocently. 'Let's take a look then,' she suggested. I followed the direction of her hand to the exam table. 'Where should we start?' she asked excitedly, just as if we were at our wedding-menu tasting. She wasn't attractive, and now that she'd stepped outside the light her whole body had dimmed a little. But she had very nice, comforting hands. 'It's these ones,' I said unwrapping the green scarf with orange duck beaks from around my neck and sliding the collar of my shirt down a little. It's worth pointing out that I have an unconventional chest – inherited from my mother – with eight ruddy moles, shapeless and of varying size. These moles are not dainty moles. Three are clustered together in a primitive constellation like a pointy triangle at the base of my neck, a little off to the left. The other five look like someone shook them in a dice cup and scattered them on my chest. They're not a pretty sight, but I've had them since I was ten years old and I know for sure that they're harmless. Mom had had them looked at – at a private clinic, of course – and the doctor in question had assured us that my moles and I would live peaceably until the end of my days. The dermatologist lifted her hands to my collarbone. Both hands. A couple of fingers alighted, smooth as a seaplane. I pictured her in bed, touching me in that gentle and focused way, determined and skillful. Her fingers circled my moles like inquisitive creatures around an intruder of unknown species. They tugged my skin flat, then released it, and carefully fondled the moles' granular surface . . . wait a second. Was she actually fondling my moles? Without gloves? She was – she was touching them! I went into a state of shock. Not even I touched my moles with such intent. They were pretty unappealing. Did she not realize this? My sister had bullied me about them for most of my childhood, claiming that nobody would ever want me, that they'd turn huge and hairy like a cow's, that I'd have to wear a turtleneck to get anyone to fall in love with me and they'd still run away the moment they discovered my secret, leaving me all alone. For the rest of my life. 'You've got no choice but to become a nun,' she'd asserted somberly. I think she might have actually believed it. Unsung childhood trauma. Her words ate away at my liver until one day, she got moles too, on the inside of her arm, redder and bulgier than mine. For a few months, I had faith in the power of the mind – I'd infected her with them! I don't think I've ever been happier than the day her moles grew to the same size as mine, then kept growing until they were nearly twice as big. Next to them, my moles were shy little girls. Hers, on the other hand, reared up on pinker skin, like strange, cerise sand castles in ruins. One summer, they started to peel. We were sitting on towels at the edge of the pool playing cards when I screamed, 'Look!' then pointed at the largest mole, covered in a crust that looked like powdered sugar. She ran over to Mom, who comforted her and said they'd go see the doctor again. The doctor corroborated his previous diagnosis: totally harmless. Still, as a teenager, my sister had her moles removed. For psychological reasons, apparently. For similar reasons, I opted to keep mine. And there I was, ready to weaponize them. The dermatologist brought her lighted magnifying glass to my chest and lingered there a while, her face centimeters from my breasts, my head thrown back to keep out of her way. I could feel her breathing, I could feel her drawing oxygen from my pores and exhaling it as carbon dioxide, hot and heavy with viruses endemic to her bronchial tree. It occurred to me that inspections like this could be as infectious as an erotic encounter. 'You don't have to worry about these moles,' she said. She'd drawn away and sat before me on a swivel stool, legs wide, ready to get to the bottom of things. 'How about we give you a general look-see while you're here?' A general look-see? That was not a medical term. The woman was so sweet, she didn't deserve to find out about my cancerous cells. 'Go on, take your shirt off so I can check your back.' It would have looked suspicious to refuse. I considered rolling up my shirt, bending over myself, and cradling my secret like a newborn while the doctor played with her magnifying glass, then getting shyly dressed and taking off before it was too late. I mean, too late for her and for her innocence, which was probably still intact. I did as she asked, and she ruled out the moles on my back. 'There are a lot of them, but they're all perfectly normal,' she assured me. Perfectly normal. If the moles on my back could become permanent to such an unnatural degree without questioning themselves, why couldn't I? 'Let's check your belly.' Belly, what belly? I turned to her. It was clear I was going to have to say something about my melanoma before she pegged me for an idiot. My mother and my sister were the only women I could bear to think of me as an idiot. 'I've had this special mole for a while but it's never bothered me.' Special? Eight in the morning, a perfect moment for dumb observations. I couldn't get out of it in the end. I felt bad for her. She would just have to diagnose me and refer me on to someone else. I focused my attention on the plant. Did she water it herself, or did the janitors? It looked like an African violet – stiff, meaty leaves, a coat of almost pubescent fuzz and buds fair and tough like cherry pits. 'This?' she asked, fondling the skin around the mole and pulling it up to the magnifying glass. Yes, I thought as I tried to make the flowers bloom from a distance. 'Oh, this is nothing. Still, you should have them looked at – like the rest of them – at least once every couple of years.' I let my head fall forward, stared at my stomach, and pointed at the shooting-star mole, thick with black, clearly cancerous suckerfish. 'This thing here is nothing?' I couldn't believe it. 'No. Nothing at all. Though if you don't like it for aesthetic reasons, we can make an appointment to have it removed.' And all of a sudden, the inside of my head began to teem with flowers pink, purple and blue. ■

© LIA D'AGOSTINO
Prayer for America
Oakland, California, 2015

I'VE BEEN AWAY FOR A WHILE

Dan Shurley

I've been away for a while. I'm meeting Kelly in the park. She's sitting among the chess players. Her new boyfriend plays chess in this park but he isn't here today. She tells me a story. 'So this guy at a party came up to me and shook my hand and he said: "Are your hands always this clammy?" And I said "I don't know." And he asked me, "Do you feel guilty about something?" And I said "I don't know!" Then he just walked off.' We see Eddy, fresh out of rehab, leaving a church. Soon he'll be crashing bar conversations outside Dahlak (he can't afford to drink inside), telling people, 'I gig.' (Press him for venues and dates and he'll cite the wedding shower he played in Bensalem in '97.) Radwan is sitting on his porch reading from his phone. The news from Syria can't be good. I can hear the social worker enunciating loudly inside; Radwan's son has autism, he's not hard of hearing. Behind the Plexiglas at Lucky's the bored proprietor is sitting and scowling. Luke's back in Philly for a few days, then he flies to Mexico City for a gig with one of the trendy synth acts he produces. I tell him to bring Eddy. He gigs. I ask Kelly if she heard the refinery explosion, the big one, the one that sparked the fire that compelled the mayor to issue a shelter-indoors warning for the neighborhoods downwind of it. 'Yeah, it woke me up that morning,' she says. 'The sky was all orange. I thought God had woken me up to witness a beautiful morning. Then I went back to bed.'

My people are exulting in hard-earned spring. The pages are flapping in the wind. The gardeners who spent the winter devising ambitious plans for cramped divisions of earth are bent over their gardens. The caution tape is skipping rope. The punctured balloons that snagged on the knuckles of trees are flapping in the cleansing wind. I should have been here transforming with the seasons, planting a bundle of keys to old apartments in the thawing earth. I should have been out back of Dahlak with Kevin, sitting on lawn chairs, chain-smoking, entertaining offers of left shoes from hapless street peddlers, giving out cigarettes like alms. Ada's taken up this life, Kevin's old life. His friends – Maisey, Jim – have become her friends. The books he read, his *Ulysses*, his *Dubliners*, his Beckett, his Burroughs, the late hours he kept, she's taken it all on. Or was she always his double?

Luke looks sleazier than I remember him, and it's not just the dollar-sign-bedizened baseball cap he's wearing. Ross is tired from the heat, tired of looking for work. We make plans to see a Derek Jarman film at International House later that night. Omar's passed on to the Great Suburb in the Sky. The soiled steps to the unmarked bar above Abyssinia, from which he would heckle bland Penn students, are quiet and clear of obstructions. The baristas at Green Line don't remember me. The clerk at Mariposa who scans my groceries doesn't remember me. Tim's introduced us five or six times. 'Didn't Tim conduct your wedding?' I ask. Now he pretends to remember me.

I walk out during the scene in the film where a punk dangling from a noose comes back to life as a yuppie, leaving Ross and Luke without a ride home. Fuck Derek Jarman and fuck Ross for not putting enough time on the meter. If I hadn't walked out I would have gotten a ticket. I drive back to the sublet. Ada's visiting. I can hear her and Lia yakking away from the open bedroom window. I'm not ready to talk to anyone. I walk to the park at the end of the city. A woman who lives on the corner greets me. I don't return the greeting. I part traffic with my indifference to death. A family's having a cookout on the terrace of a house next to the barbershop. The red-and-white pole of the barbershop is spinning, trip-hop is the soundtrack to the flowering feeling up on the terrace. The light turns green. 'It's me, your Uncle Fester,' someone jokes. I remember that they stop checking the meter after eight on that stretch of Chestnut. Ross did put enough time on the meter.

The priest at my brother's funeral assured us he was up there in heaven with Jimi Hendrix, hearing the latest music before it reaches us, discussing elements of style and composition with other dead artists. He knew nothing about the young man who hanged himself beyond the obituary I wrote, but what did I know? I claimed him for myself, describing him as a seeker who'd studied art (he dropped out after one semester). So the priest improvised. Talking feedback. Guitar pick. Heaven is a recording studio where time is limitless. I feel cold. Gather round the burning bush. Gather round the hole it leaves. The German film crew is here. They want to know everything.

Ada texts Lia to invite us to join her over at Dahlak for a drink. She's with Maisey, who just got out of the hospital, or rehab, or was thrown out of another group house, raped, hospitalized. I don't know if I'm getting the timeline right. I wouldn't be surprised if she's sitting at the bar in a hospital gown. She was there among the faces hanging off our table when I was last in town for my brother's funeral, one of the girls who was in love with Kevin. In my grief I saw everything clearly, how Kevin was surrounded by scroungers who would pull him down. I didn't know he was already down, that these were his people, and that I'd be returning for his funeral two years later. We get dressed, down some mescal and make our way toward the bar. We see Ada and Maisey sitting out back. They don't notice us passing through the parking lot on our way to the park for people with fallen homies (per Lia's lexicon). There's an oak tree in the park that reminds me of Kevin. It has a gaping hole in its trunk where one of its huge boughs broke off.

When the Pages Are Flapping

When the pages are flapping I am happy. When the pages are flapping I'm not worried about the child climbing the dormant electric fence. When the pages are flapping I cease lamenting the fate of the ostracized lover. When the pages are flapping I don't care what happens to the American tourist abducted by terrorists and sold into sexual slavery. When the pages are flapping I don't lose sleep over the soul of the murderer. I've been told to stop. I could go on. I will go on. When the pages are flapping the smog of fried chicken is lifted. Dark pink flowers bloom with orange doodads. Nooses revert back to hardened vines. When the pages are flapping nothing is at stake because everything is already lost, and the pages breathe freely in their textlessness.

Please take a moment to appreciate the pages flapping.

'They're trying to outsmart this ludicrous magistrate who wears a three-cornered hat. And that symbolizes his pompousness, the three-cornered hat.' Ross listens to classical music on the radio as he works. Copyediting a client's Orientalist novel, tutoring a Saudi princeling, applying for teaching jobs, his own novel in the back of the drawer. 'Uncomfortable for sure, that high humidity, and watch out for those torrential downpours. Up next we have a quartet of saxophones . . .' After spending a year in Vienna on a Fulbright, he has yet to reconcile with his old life. He curses the surge of strung-out panhandlers on the streets, laments the absence of multigenerational families picnicking in parks at night. In any case, his preferred habitat is no city but a stuffed brown chair facing an air conditioner.

Some people in Cedar Park held a candlelight vigil for Lucky's, the Chinese takeout joint that closed when their rent was doubled. I saw the stories and tributes circulating on Facebook. 'Where else am I going to get fried tofu at 2 a.m.?' Tim posted. Five years ago, when I lived across the street from Lucky's, I wrote a poem about the owner.

> When I entered he rose up from his dinner and went
> behind the Plexiglas to take my order. 'One egg roll,' he
> repeated, slashing pictographs onto a piece of cardboard.
> His dull limbs awaited my next move. 'That's it?' 'That's
> it,' I said. He turned stiffly in the direction of the kitchen
> and squinted. The smuggler's fee, the store, the green
> card, the wife and children, naturalization. Was it worth
> it? Standing behind a Plexiglas wall fourteen hours a day
> seven days a week dropping egg rolls singly into boiling oil?

The owner was gruff to the point of rudeness. We have a long tradition of steak sandwich slingers and deli countermen abusing customers in this city, so the Lucky's guy made sense to us. Once I saw him smile. He was out with his wife, his infant daughter bobbing on his chest. They had stopped to browse Tim's junk sale. Unobscured by the greasy Plexiglas, his wife was radiant. Tim recognized him and they exchanged a few words. He smiled. He was clearly in love with his baby.

Lucky's will inevitably be replaced by a restaurant that closes at 10 p.m. The food will be better and more expensive. It will be rationally managed and staffed by young people selected for their obsequiousness and perpetual smiles, as dogs were selected by our early ancestors.

Over dinner – fake kielbasa, sauerkraut, garlic mustard – Kelly reports that the toxicity of the chemicals released into the air by the refinery explosion was worse than the company and city has admitted, according to two university reports. 'But it's not like any of us were outside for more than ten minutes,' she says, alluding to some sociological study. 'I work outside,' Ada reminds her. It's true, she works at a cemetery. Nowhere near the refinery. 'Dan's dad works at the refinery,' Lia reminds them, 'He drove right into the fireball.' I laugh. I notice I'm hunched over my plate like my dad. When I called him to see if he was OK I ended up breaking the news to him. He'd been off that day. He told me he'd call and see what was going on. The next day he was aping the company's PR: 'It was never a problem the hydrofluoric acid they use was in containment before it happened it was a butane tank that exploded it could have been worse . . .' The following day he went back to work. If the explosion had killed a dozen people he would have still gone back to work.

He works through the night unloading barrels of oil at the refinery. He is old, defeated, drugged, destroyed by the death of his youngest son, his movements are economical, his face fixed in a sneer. The oldest man on the job, he works out of a defensive crouch. And he works carefully, as carefully as he held me in his hands when I was a baby. My father used to laugh at the metal splinters in his hands, because pain was certainty then, and certainty love. The splinters that made him give up two-part inventions for the organ and his dream of becoming a professional musician. He unloads the oil from the freight train with great care, because my life is in his hands. Now he laughs nervously. Will the oil keep flowing? Three more years. That's all he needs. Then he can retire. When the world releases him from its oily grip will there still be a world?

'The Sunrise Coalition said we shouldn't blame the workers,' Kelly says, sanctimoniously repeating the activist group's statement. No, let's not blame the workers. After all, they make the gasoline that moves your car, the car that affords you privacy and security as you inch along the Schuylkill in rush-hour traffic through the maze of overpasses, the wreckage of blown tires, past the polygonal facade of the Amtrak building that magnifies the anemic sun and warms your face on a winter day as you sit in your beat-up old Volvo, gassed up and daydreaming about waterskiing. Let's not blame the workers. 'Wow, this is a real bummer of a dinner conversation,' Ada observes. 'Are you kidding me?' I say. 'This is political gold! We're the folks sitting around the kitchen table! Steve can't put food on the table because the refinery shut down. Steve's just trying to feed his family. He's got a pulmonary embolism, he's prediabetic and will probably lose his foot if he doesn't get it checked out soon. Steve shouldn't have to sacrifice his health to provide for his family!' Kelly watches as I load more of her sauerkraut onto my bun. I take another big bite. The gesture feels working class.

A Brief Biography of My Father
(The Early Middle Years)

1977. His hair is long and wavy and golden. He's scowling like a young lion for the wedding photographer. 1981. Now smiling sheepishly at the eight-pound infant nestled in his sinewy forearm. A son! It'll be a few more years until it's my turn to yowl, to take my first out-breath, give my first lowing wail.

He bounds down the stairs in the morning on his way to the plant, taking the last three at a leap and landing with a thud that shakes the brittle porcelain bells in the landlady's china closet. Returning from work, his face drained of color and enthusiasm, with just enough energy left to make it up the stairs, the landlady intercepts him at the landing. 'Steve, I know it's you running down the stairs in the morning, and I would appreciate it if you didn't do that anymore.' This is the way most adults talk to him, with a mixture of disappointment and admonishment, depending on how much he owes them. They all sound like the voice he makes when he's imitating his father, an IRS accountant, giving him tax advice.

He is the last in a line of anonymous appendages to power stretching at least as far back as the sixteenth century (a distant ancestor served as treasurer to Henry VIII). The line does not include him: he is its terminus. No, he is the origin of an awkward, fledgling new line.

Their first apartment is too small to accommodate the organ. It sits in his parents' garage. After a while his fingertips stop anticipating the supple weight of the keys pressing up against them.

In the early morning in the shower the swirl of voices bubbles up and he bursts forth with bits of Jimi Hendrix solos, jingles, odd phrases, goaty ululations, imitations, sounds of machines whirring and stamping metal parts, like a cipher repeating the sounds he's heard the previous day. This manic stream of sounds spreads into the halls of his apartment building where, apart from the steam and reverberation that give it the swell of music, it becomes all too intelligible. He steps out into the now silent hall and quietly makes his way down the stairs.

1986. Another infant cradled in his arm, this one a girl, born with broken hips and the cord wrapped around her throat. His little girl. A miracle she survived. His hair is short and he sports a green-gold mustache. My father is beginning to assume his recognizable form.

1991. A fat baby boy perched on his paunch. His hair is cut very short, his upper lip bare. He is born again.

Four sets of eyes peer out at us from behind a tree trunk. 'We're trying to scratch the wood off this tree,' one of the boys explains to us as we pass. 'But it's wood all over,' I say. Kelly and I continue walking, neither of us remarking on the absence of adult supervision. After a few paces I hear the boldest boy say, 'You're right.' We're walking the trail that runs along Cobbs Creek on the border of Philadelphia and my hometown. I was warned to stay away from this park, but some older kids were always cutting a hole in the fence. We played in cars that had been abandoned, stripped for parts and burned. When the creek froze the chemical run off in the water made rainbows on the surface.

A few weeks ago, Kelly tells me, two of her neighbors were shot. A pregnant woman and the man who threw his body in front of her. They were shot by a vengeful ex-lover with a semiautomatic rifle. 'Blap blap blap blap' is the sound the gun made. She doesn't reproduce the screams. The screams are implied. The man had helped her move a piece of furniture just the day before.

We hear the sound of basketballs thudding as we approach Baltimore Avenue. The trolley muscles around the Caribbean restaurant with a screech as it eases into its final resting place. On the basketball court a boy maneuvers a remote-controlled car under the legs of the men jockeying for position under the netless rim.

This city is filled with wrecks like us. Wrecks who are filled with the wreckage of others. The good news is the ambulance and fire department are already here in case any of these fireworks turn out to be lethal projectiles lofted on the wings of pistols. Don't say I never loved. I loved even the ominous bells, the wet limestone after a sunshower and the pale yellow light, the vague rainbow (an oil slick in the sky?). The hem of Lia's dress brushing the hairs of my leg. Cuz mother moon scraped it elegant that night, yeah.

One of These Mornings

Sweep sweep. Yawny greetings shouted across the narrow street. Kids playing on the porch next door, the screen door screeching as the adults come and go. The children are making tiny siren sounds, tiny strafing sounds. Well then, what are we waiting for? More explosions. Did we run out already?

The emissary from Amazon beeps and blips, scans the goods, sends her coordinates back to the mothership. A spry old man waves goodbye. I can't tell if the figure sitting on the couch across the way is a statue or an old woman, she's sitting so still. I take another sip of my coffee and let the record skip. The neighbors' screen door, at first alarmingly unhinged, now sounds more like an elbow creak. Someone pounding chicken in the kitchen. The glockenspiels are quiet on this Bastille Day weekend. I stop the record and turn on the radio. Ravel: 'impressionistic *and* modern'. Out of the corner of my eye the statue puts on a hat.

They ripped out the trees at City Hall and installed a water park, glass ramps, a Starbucks in a glass box. Those trees were the last vestige of the city's sanity! They sheltered homeless people and birds. It will take a century for the new trees to provide any cover. The government buildings, however, are as opaque as ever. They flattened Love Park. The new fountain is a flaccid version of its predecessor. Without the concentric seating that gave the park the feel of street theater it's a traffic island. I take the 32 through the museum district, past wide boulevards narrowing into rows of cramped houses, an untouched row of rental bikes arranged along a weedy lot, to the ragged edge of Fairmount Park. I step down to have a look around. The faces are darker, the houses are taller, wider and in poorer repair. Victorians the color of dried blood with cataracts and missing teeth, a driving range on the edge of the park, a half-demolished warehouse with a huge sign bearing the smiling face of a white real estate agent, and past that, a bridge spanning a maze of transformers and pylons; coiled metal effigies to the old gods of industry, steaming in the drizzle. A man walking in the rain holds a triangle hat of newspaper over his head. The sidewalk dissolves into mud. This neighborhood has the wideness, the flatness, and the moldering indifference of the South.

Cousin Mary's house is boarded up. Newspaper clippings in the windows announce a commemorative event long passed.

On the 35th Anniversary of the MOVE* Bombing

The MOVE house was situated smack in the middle of a block with a view of Cobbs Creek Park. The houses the city let burn to the ground were replaced with squared-off contraptions that look uninhabited to this day, houses designed to be so uninspiring as to never allow a utopian idea to ever take root again. But there it is, the forest at the end of the city. With the sun going down it beckons you, you could get lost in that forest and come out feeling like you belong to the land and how to build a life around that feeling?

I sit on the steps of the boarded-up house watching the city workers teeing off on their lunch break. Before he made *Giant Steps*, Coltrane took small steps in Philly. He walked to the Jewish deli. He took the trash out. He pulled up some weeds in the garden in back of Cousin Mary's house. He kicked heroin. He practiced throughout the day and night, his horn rippling the lawns of Fairmount Park, protector of the Schuylkill. Gigs on Columbia Ave to stay sharp. He would still be practicing backstage just before it was time to go on so that the first phrase out of his horn flowed like the middle of a conversation. He gets home still whirling but exhausted – no, not exhausted, he hasn't yet exhausted the possibilities of the horn. Soon he'll put the in-breath to work too.

And you realize that Exodus is the name of a woman. And how enduringly the day dies, the city burns the movement to the ground, the saxophonist throws down his horn and screams. Give us the ashes then. The coffee grinds, the dregs of your choice wine, we'll take all of it. Grow something where. Build something in. My dead are many and near. I hear them in the tall grasses. My dear friends are here, and the house where Coltrane drove his neighbors crazy with his devotion. The house still stands.

The person who lives above us is crying like they just lost a member of their tribe. The sobbing is sad enough, but when they start kicking at the floor I want to knock on their door and try to console them. But I don't. I stick to my training and leave them alone with their pain. Yet I can't help feeling connected to them now. We grieve on parallel planes. They writhe around on the floor and I beat my head with a book. Lia dashes a mug on the wall and screams, and I sweep up the broken shards without saying a word, like a bartender clearing the empties before setting up the next round.

At 3 a.m. the smoke detector requests a new battery. It continues chirping after I take out the dying battery. I rip it out of the wall and it protests louder. I would throw it against the wall, but we're subletting, and we already destroyed one of the girl's mugs. So I get dressed and set out for the 24-hour CVS on foot. Fog moistening the streets. Trolley tracks cooling. The people I dodged all day, gone. Conversations lilt down from hidden balconies. I walk unencumbered by traffic, crossing wherever. I'm convinced that if Kevin were alive I would run into him. He, using up the night and me, observing the nocturnal life like a visitor to a foreign country. The CVS is staggeringly bright and empty. I don't see the clerk who supervises the machines, but I hear her singing somewhere in the store. The grace of automation: no one asks me, 'How's your night going?'

I wake from fitful sleep to the sight of a thick wall of orange clouds curdling above the rows of houses. For a moment I don't know where I am. California after an earthquake? Florida during an eclipse? I pull the curtain closed but my mind is spinning, I can't fall back to sleep. The clouds beckon me out into the street. I put on pants, shoes, check myself in the mirror. My eyes are steel sinks not wet with rest, hair a thatch of macheted weeds. I walk out into the street just as I am, jaundiced and craggy with troubled sleep, expecting the wall of clouds I saw from my window to have been a mirage, expecting comforting darkness. But it's light out, painfully bright, the clouds seem to be illuminated from within. I've been away for a while but I know these streets better than I know myself. But I've never seen a sunrise like this before. No one should be seeing this, I think. We must not know how insane we really are. Dreaming under the spell of these clouds that don't cast shadows and whose light is a delirium. We're wise to stay inside sleeping, or we observe a prohibition we never had to be told. Where are the clouds leading me? The gardeners are away from their gardens. The caution tape is skipping rope for no jumpers. The trolleys don't clank and vibrate the wooden slats of park benches pressed against the aching backs of homeless people. The bars are sullen, unsentinel, the vapors of false communion dissolved by the first rays of light. The church bells don't toll for fear of waking the sleepers who would be drawn out into the street by the sight of this beckoning God road. The clouds stretched over the roofs glow with the homing instinct of all sentient beings to converge, to be together whatever, it's as beatific and unsettling as anything I've ever dreamed. So where is everyone? Where are the wanderers incompletely consumed by fire? Where are the addicts with hot metal in their chests, with eyes and lips and lungs and fingertips burned on pipes? Where are the hungry ghosts? Where are the nurses on their way to work? Where is Kevin? The clouds are moving on, dispersing, the streets graying in their absence. In the drab gray awake I see the yellow residue of streetlights in the eyes of daisies, see my jaundiced reflection in the daisies. The sky no longer beckons as it did from my room. The wall of clouds isn't for climbing. I'll never reach the horizon, which is not a Great Wall or an Ark or the apocalypse around the corner but another horizon. And just before the clouds disappear into the blue of day as though they never existed, I see him walking.

He's just climbed down from those deathless clouds. He's just burned off the last traces of the night that was his balm. To be with us again, to fail with us again, to sound out the limit of his existence again. The screaming is over. His speakers are blown. I watch him glide along walls warming with sunlight, like a holy man trailing robes not yet visible, a hand covering the static whispering from his mouth. Kevin, I want to say, but he might not recognize me in this form. Or his face will soften with recognition. And I will know that this is the end. And I know that nothing ends. I watch him walking toward the Agony House, a prayer pressed to his burnt lips. Where he sits on the porch smoking his last cigarette.

When we get to the rehearsal at Elise's place everyone is plastered. Elise is giving Therese's walker a lap dance. Therese's breasts keep spilling out over her jumpsuit as she jerks her banged-up body up and down. She was struck by a car while getting off a bus. She apologizes for flashing everyone. Tim pours red wine into mugs and hands them to us. We have to drink fast to catch up or wilt into the background. I wilt into the background. Elise lives in a subsidized artist's loft with central air. Being here in a heatwave feels regal. The room goes quiet when Erin starts singing in her deep, croaky voice while Ross provides angular piano accompaniment from the back room. Erin plays the mother to Elise's child. We sit in reverent silence as she channels deep pain, caressing Elise's real childhood wounds (both her parents committed suicide when she was an infant). In Elise's play the child born with a blue birthmark is the cause of her mother's death. Joel plays the father who resents the child's existence. Erin spills a full mug of red wine down her shirt, mumbles something about medical marijuana and PTSD. We dance sensually (Elise), absurdly (Ross), cadaverously (Jim). As the party thins out Elise becomes needier. She's leaving for Prague for a month to study puppet making or something. She makes it sound like she's going into exile. Lia wants to hang out more but I'm tired and ready to go home. Elise finds my reserve threatening and demands I show my cards: do I think she's annoying or something? I know where this is going. Elise's boyfriend sits on the couch waiting patiently for us to leave so he can drink alone.

We're sitting on the worn limestone steps of the closed pet shop. Apparently it's a holiday. Lia stops a woman in black who is walking a black dog with brown paws. 'Can we pet your dog?' she asks. Out comes Lemon Pie's purple tongue, but the dog is too afraid to get any closer to us. 'We found her in a field in Mississippi. The rescue drove her up here,' the woman says. She lifts the dog by her barrel chest to show her the cats in the window. Lemon Pie is unimpressed. Now Ada wants to move to Mississippi, where chows – 'the best kind of dog!' – can be found in fields. Lia wants not the state but the dog with the anxiety problem, like our other pets. 'I want to move back to the South again,' says another dog walker passing by at that moment, her outer-thigh tattoos winking back at us. 'Not Charlotte again. Maybe Asheville.'

'Let's move to the country,' the next singer up on the barista's playlist whisper-warbles, and the buoyant mood in the cafe dies. I just came from the country. Nothing happens in the fucking country. I want to be here!

I help Jim break down Tim's curb sale, a show of camaraderie, almost out of spite. Jim is the head groundskeeper at the cemetery where he and Ada work. When I texted to ask him if they needed any help he deferred and deflected and then hired Elise. I'm so broke I'd work the graveyard shift at the graveyard. Go home and read Beckett. Strap me into bed and blindfold me. Tim returns to A-Space in jolly spirits, his breath reeking of alcohol, with croissants (chocolate and almond paste!) and challah bread that's supposed to go to Food Not Bombs. (Note to readers considering applying for public assistance: don't put 'Food Not Bombs' as current food source on the application. The word 'bombs' is a red flag and will trigger the dreaded personal interview.) As I'm putting croissants in my bag a big Jamaican with bloodshot eyes walking a Rottweiler pup stops to chat with us. Tim offers him a loaf of challah. He wants the one with raisins, not eggs. 'Raisins! Not eggs! One love!' I can't tell if he's playing a Jamaican or not. Fist bumps all around.

On a whim I knock on Radwan's door. He invites me in. I go upstairs to grab my guitar and ask Lia if she wants to join us. We go back down together. Radwan has his son Hamudi sit next to me on the couch. Hamudi plucks the bass string of my guitar and watches it ring out, mesmerized, then laughs maniacally and runs away. He keeps trying to flash us and once succeeds. Radwan tries to contain him and Hamudi slaps him in the face. 'No, thank you,' Radwan says. This is what the social worker advised him to do in these situations. Lia thinks the boy has a crush on me and is mad at his dad for cock-blocking. But he forgets his anger when Radwan tickles him. A pubescent boy who cannot speak, whose every movement is controlled, no wonder he rages for hours on end.

Since Shanaz is in bed with a pinched nerve, Radwan makes tea and serves us cashews and Shanaz's fig-stuffed cookies. He gets very sad when we talk about the crisis in Syria. Lia changes the subject to the new neighbors. They vacuum at least three times a day. 'They must worship their vacuum cleaner,' she says. Shanaz laughs from the bedroom and puts in a biblical quip. Radwan translates and we laugh as though we've understood.

At night, when the watchful gaze of our temporary neighbors turns inward, to their big screens, and the vegetation-cloaked trail along Cobbs Creek reverts to campground for the unhoused, and the cars careening around the parkway loosen up because the lights are green and farther ahead turning green, and a jacked-up day laborer buying a forty of malt liquor at the beer store says, 'It's me, your Uncle Fester,' and the cat is lounging on the bed belly up, and it's cool enough to give the A/C a rest, and I've just talked to Peter in San Francisco for two hours and handed him over to Lia, and the work is as done as it's going to get, I stand in front of the full-length mirrors that flank the bed, my head glittering gold, my eyes bloodshot from happiness, the black hollows under my eyes black with joy, trimming the stray hairs around my nipples.

Dear friends: I've been away for a while. Now I must leave again. I take a walk around the block. Scaffolding crowding the steps of the church where I usually sit. A man hunched over, hands in head, head in hands, counting his remaining teeth. Sir, if I could have just a moment of your time – Sorry. I understand. Hey, remember when. I remember everything. I'm walking behind a mother and child with a bulldog on a leash. I don't want to scare them. The mother hears leaves rattling, senses my presence, moves to the side, the girl and the dog move to the side. The girl is eight, nine. They're talking like girlfriends, the mother professing her love of books, the child her loathing. Up ahead on the corner there's a little hutch where people put unwanted books. That's where I'm headed. I overtake them. We arrive at the same place. 'Put the book in there,' the mother tells the child. She hesitates, afraid of me. 'Do you have another book to add?' I ask her. She smiles shyly and places it on the pile. The mother's deep-set features are in shadows. She has only books and the conversation of her young child. Under the streetlight I can see that she's smiling sadly. They move on. The book is called *The Care of the Soul*. File under self-help, or whatever they call it now. The cover is sticky with little-girl hands and dog drool. I leave it for someone else and keep walking to the park for people with fallen homies. The grass is tall and thick. The benches are all occupied. Silent tears are streaming from the cataracted eyes of a drunk sitting on the edge of a park bench. Two men with neat dreads are taking big rips of weed, blunt guts at their feet. They're laughing as they trade stories about a mutual friend in the past tense. I pass a couple clinging tightly to each other under a blanket. Down in the bowl I see flashlights, a crowd of people have gathered to listen to a woman strumming a guitar. With a ragged, reaching voice she sings: *Are you thinking about love or are you thinking about yourself?* Hey, remember when Jimi gave us rainbows and Janis took a piece of our heart? Janis is urging us on to greater heights of selfless love from the declivity of a dark green oasis in a maddening city. The year is 2018. The basketballs raining down on the court are thinking about love. The drunk with tears streaming down his face is thinking about love. The gaping hole in the giant oak tree is thinking about love. The hole is shaped just like the sound hole of a guitar. Down in the bowl the flashlights are twirling and jumping with joy. Everyone unremembering the chains of trauma that brought them into being, that root them to benches and grooves in the sidewalk with dandelions pressed between their toes. My back aches. I sit on the downed tree limb to think about love. The song ends. The people in the bowl applaud, the basketballs raining down on the court applaud, the drunk with tears streaming down his face applauds, I applaud. And then a directorial voice issues from the bowl: 'OK, actors. Go home.' ∎

---

*EDITOR'S NOTE: The revolutionary Black liberation and animal rights organization, MOVE, was founded in 1972 in Philadelphia. The group, which opposed all governmental and capitalist structures, police brutality and modern technology, were evicted by force in 1978. A police officer was killed during the armed siege, and nine members of the group – one of whom was heavily pregnant – were sentenced to life in prison. (They assert that the officer was killed by police shooting behind him.) In 1985, a second eviction and armed stand-off involving 500 police officers ended when a police helicopter bombed the MOVE house on Osage Avenue with a so-called 'entry device'. Six adults and five children died in the ensuing fire, and sixty-five houses were destroyed. Survivor Ramona Africa and relatives of the deceased filed a civil suit, and were awarded $1.5 million in a 1996 settlement. Displaced residents were awarded $12.83 million in damages in 2005, following a jury trial.

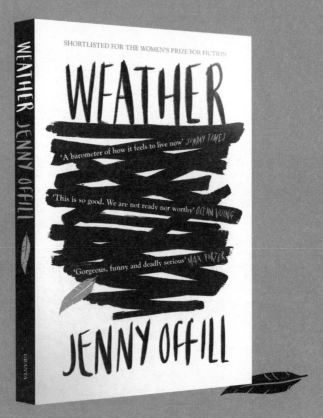

Detail of St Rollox Works from *Bird's Eye View of Glasgow*, *Illustrated London News*, 26 March 1864
Image courtesy of the University of Glasgow Library

THE STINKY OCEAN

Ian Jack

1. Under the clouds

I left home in Fife and went to live in Glasgow when I was eighteen. When I think of it now, the distance seems laughably small – forty miles, little more than an hour in the train – but the contrast between a village on the east coast and a city, Scotland's largest, on the west coast was sharp and exciting. I had a bedsit in a dark street of better-class tenements, with a Polish delicatessen, a dance hall and a cinema just round the corner. Glasgow seemed an infinite place, never to be known completely no matter how many suburban bus terminals you reached or exploratory walks you made. It was 1963. The last trams had run the year before, but the city was still much its old self – smoke-blackened, run-down, Victorian, majestic, tipsy on beer and whisky on a Saturday night, hushed on a Sunday. More than a million people lived there then; forty years later, that figure had almost halved.

In the first months I went home with my washing on Fridays and returned with clean clothes early on Mondays. Certain features of the journey became familiar – a working colliery or two, the extravagant facade of a psychiatric hospital half hidden by trees – but none was as mysterious as the stretch of waste ground that could be glimpsed from the carriage window just before the train reached the Glasgow terminus. It was a peculiar, alopecic landscape of hummocks and gullies, with patches of grass growing on what looked like white earth, and rarely a soul to be seen. Then in quick succession came the blackness of a tunnel, the slowing scrape of train wheels and your release into a thriving, peopled scene of shops and buses, a world away from the bit of the moon the train had trundled through only moments before.

Incongruously, prompted by the sight of Lady Anne Glenconner on Britain's most popular chat show, I remembered this long-ago scenery last autumn. Glenconner appeared on *The Graham Norton Show* to promote her book about her three decades as Princess Margaret's lady-in-waiting, its publication timed to coincide with the launch of the third season of Netflix's royal family drama, *The Crown*, in which Helena Bonham Carter plays the princess and Olivia Colman is her sister, the queen. The two actors shared the chat show's sofa with the author, who had helped Bonham Carter with her role by providing some details of the princess's behaviour. Nothing more than twenty minutes of mild gossip seemed in prospect: Glenconner was, after all, the 87-year-old daughter of an earl, the widow of a baron, a maid of honour at the queen's coronation in 1953 and a trusted courtier. But she was sensational. The audience erupted in wave after wave of laughter at her frank revelations of aristocratic tantrums and sexual misbehaviour. Helped by several more television appearances, her book became a bestseller. She gave one-woman shows in theatres and signed a contract with her publishers for two crime novels, the first to be called *Murder on Mustique*. Disclosures about the private life of royalty have been making money for British publishers since the Second World War, if not longer, and yet this book spilled few royal beans in its portrayal of Princess Margaret as a troubled and misunderstood but essentially kind woman – 'the best friend I ever had', Glenconner said – rather than the little monster of hauteur and vanity that anecdotes suggested. Instead, the book's gargoyles, the characters who cause a shudder and a gasp, are Lady Anne's husband, Colin Tennant, the 3rd Baron Glenconner, and one or two of his relations.

As a Coke (pronounced Cook), Lady Anne came from a grander family than he did – Cokes had been earls of Leicester since the eighteenth century, when the first earl, Thomas Coke, built what is generally reckoned to be the finest Palladian house in England on his 27,000-acre estate at Holkham in Norfolk. The Glenconners were upstarts by comparison. Their title, a barony, had been created in the twentieth century. Six generations previously, when Coke returned from the grand tour to set about creating his magnificent house, the Tennants were scraping a living as subsistence farmers in Ayrshire. Wealth had put their male descendants through the usual finishing schools for English gentlemen. Colin, typically, got his education at Eton and Oxford; was commissioned as an officer in the Irish Guards; and inherited a fine London house and a Scottish estate as well as a job in the family's merchant bank. Even so, Lady Anne's father, the fifth earl, considered him a mountebank. When members of the royal family joined a shooting party at Holkham, he was made to walk with the beaters.

Old money's distaste for new money was only partly to blame for his in-laws' hostility. Tennant was also known to be a libertine – a Mayfair brothel-goer who on his honeymoon took his wife to a seedy Paris hotel to watch another couple having sex ('two really disgusting people . . . squelching about, and I didn't really know what to do so I sat back in my chair and closed my eyes' was how she described the episode on Norton's show). Princess Margaret, who knew him before his marriage, described him to his bride's mother as a 'fairly decadent fellow', but decadence was only half the story. He was extravagant, capricious and wilful, and given to extraordinary tantrums, seizure-like in their sudden arrival and ferocity, which alarmed anyone unlucky enough to witness them. His temper brought an opera to a halt in Verona's amphitheatre and enraged the crowd in a Delhi bazaar. Setting out with his wife and Princess Margaret on a transatlantic flight, and refused an upgrade so that he could join them in first class, he lay down in the foetal position in the aisle of economy and wailed and screamed until security arrived and dragged him from the plane. (British Airways then banned him for life.) And his wilfulness could be expensive: he bought the Caribbean island of Mustique without setting foot on it and bought and sold homes in London at a perplexing, unprofitable rate.

There was evidence of a family trait, a genetic disposition to exhibitionism, narcissism and the most tremendous sulks. One of his Tennant uncles, Uncle Stephen, who as a Bright Young Thing could count Siegfried Sassoon and Cecil Beaton among his passionate admirers, got bored with the world and spent most of his last thirty years lying powdered, lipsticked and perfumed in bed at his large country house in Wiltshire. Late one summer, lying in another bed at the family seat in Scotland, he complained that the heather he could see from his window was 'such a vulgar shade of purple' – whereupon, according to Anne Glenconner, his nephew Colin arranged for the hillside to be strewn with thousands of paper flowers to turn purple into a pleasant shade of blue.

You need money to behave like that. Where did the money come from? A good part of the explanation lay in the Glasgow wastelands that I saw from the train. But if you were to look beyond that, to something primordial that predated human ingenuity, then the answer might be a climatic fact, something that nature had unfairly ordained, which is the shortage of direct sunlight in western Scotland. Day after day, the Atlantic weather system sweeps in grey, moist blankets of cloud; a week can go by when the pavements never dry completely and the stratus rarely lifts from the hill. It can be no coincidence that it was in Glasgow that a Glasgow man, Charles Macintosh, invented the raincoat. In 1963, as autumn turned to winter, the street outside my digs would glisten wet under the street lamps a little earlier each day, while living rooms across the way had their lights switched on by four o'clock.

2. Improbable heights

In Glasgow at that time, what the name Tennant mainly evoked was a memory of height. 'Tennant's Stalk' had been demolished in the early 1920s, but books of city history recalled it as a marvel, a chimney that at 455 feet and 6 inches tall stood higher than any other man-made structure in the world when it was completed in 1842 (except two of the pyramids at Giza and the spire of Strasbourg Cathedral). The German travel writer Johann Georg Kohl was overwhelmed by its size when he reached Glasgow in the year of its completion. 'A truly wonderful erection,' Kohl wrote, which 'rose over the city and its fog like the minster spire over Strasbourg or that of St Stephen's over Vienna.' Before he saw the city's usual attractions – its medieval cathedral and fifteenth-century university – he went straight to Tennant's chemical factory to check the chimney's officially stated height, which seemed to him 'improbable'. In fact, the height was only half the marvel. At the factory, Kohl discovered a labyrinth of underground vents that led from the factory's various departments and grew larger as they joined together, just as tributaries swell a river, until they were finally united at the chimney's base, where the draught drew their collected smoke and smells up the stalk to drift high above the Glasgow streets. Hot air is less dense than cold air and therefore rises above it: all chimneys operate on that principle. But the taller the chimney is, the greater the volume of hot air inside it will be, and the fiercer the draught or upward current. The stalk's great height gave it unprecedented drawing power. Workmen at Tennant's told Kohl that when they were sent to repair the flues and vents, they had to make sure that the doors that stood between the vents and the larger channels were tight shut before they started work. Otherwise, they found they required 'all their strength to prevent themselves being drawn in', to be sucked tumbling towards the chimney's base.

Kohl was captivated. He wondered if a similar system could be applied to whole cities, so that 'the smoke of all the houses . . . might then be conveyed, by subterranean channels, to a gigantic chimney in the neighbourhood, and there carried off.' The chimneys themselves might be designed as 'graceful and ornamental architectural monuments' rather than utilitarian smoke-expellers. It was a visionary moment of which little came. No matter how high they rose, factory chimneys rarely raised the human spirit, and Tennant's Stalk never outgrew its humble role as the exhaust of smoke and fumes from what, when the chimney was built, was said to be the largest chemical works in Europe, perhaps the world.

Most of this was the achievement of Charles Tennant, an Ayrshire farmer's son, though luck and loot as well as energy and intellectual curiosity had played a part. His father, John Tennant, had been lucky as a young man to know a servant girl, Elizabeth Maguire, who worked on his father's farm at Alloway. Maguire had been lucky to have a childless uncle, James Macrae, the son of an Ayr washerwoman, who rose through the East India Company to become president (governor) of the Madras Presidency. Macrae had been lucky – the standard luck of the British ruler-cum-trader in eighteenth-century India – and he came home with a fortune that was typically opaque in its origins. An extensive inquiry by the East India Company cleared him of corruption, though, in the words of the *Dictionary of National Biography*, 'the relationships between all the proponents were extremely complicated, involving as they did relationships between Britons acting on their own and on the company's behalf, Britons transacting with Indian merchants on both accounts, and Indian merchants dealing among themselves.' Returned to Ayr after his long absence, he bought several estates and settled dowries on his nieces. When he died, Elizabeth Maguire inherited his estate at Ochiltree and £45,000 in diamonds, which made her attractive to the 13th Earl of Glencairn. As the Countess Glencairn, she needed a new estate manager or factor and found him in her childhood friend John Tennant, who in 1769 moved with his wife and children to their new home, Glenconner farm, where, as well as managing the estate, he leased 139 acres of farmland for his own use.

Tennant believed that literacy was the key to progress. Before he moved to Glenconner, he and a neighbouring farmer, William Burnes, sent their children to a progressive little school where they read Milton and Dryden; one of Burnes's children, the poet Robert Burns, became a family friend. But literacy introduced rural families to more profitable ways of making a living as well as to poetry. Tennant became an agricultural improver, enclosing and draining land, and planting it with potatoes and turnips to supplement the oats that were Scotland's traditional crop. Two sources of income, farming as well as factoring, meant he could afford to prolong his sons' education into their teens, widening their horizons from the prospect of a life spent labouring in the family fields. One became an evangelist in India; another joined the Royal Navy; others migrated to Ireland and Cape Town. Charles Tennant, his sixth child (he had sixteen in all), left home aged fifteen to start his apprenticeship as a handloom weaver in the village of Kilbarchan, near the textile-manufacturing town of Paisley.

This was propitious. The Scottish textile industry was beginning to grow at an exciting rate, thanks to fresh capital investment, increasing imports of cheap cotton fibre from India and the Caribbean, and new manufacturing techniques. Output of cotton and linen fabrics soared, and would have soared more but for a bottleneck further down the production line: bleaching. Textiles need to be bleached; as well as whitening the cloth, bleaching cleans it and prepares it for dyeing. The traditional method had changed very little since the age of the toga and its cycle could take up a whole summer. Cloth was steeped in a weak alkaline solution (sometimes urine and water) for several days, and then washed and spread out in the open air for several weeks; the process was repeated half a dozen times before a last steeping, this time in sour milk, after which the cloth would be washed clean again and spread out to dry for a final time.

The spreading out, known as 'crofting', took up space as well as time, occupying large stretches of ground that might have been used more profitably. And the Scottish sun could never be relied on: bleaching by sunlight was one thing on the banks of the Nile, the Ganges and the Euphrates, or even the Tiber or the Seine, but quite another on the Clyde, which often has less than half the annual sunshine of seaside resorts only 400 miles away in southern England. 'It is a pity that a country so charming as Scotland should not be favoured with a finer climate,' wrote the travel writer Kohl on his upriver journey to see Tennant's Stalk, unaware of the distant connection between the climate and the chimney.

3. As infernal as any earthly place

In Anne Glenconner's memoir the word *bleach* is mentioned only once. In the context of her father's resolute snobbery, she writes that while the Coke fortune could be traced to the fifteenth century and sprang from law and land, 'the Tennant family had made its – albeit vast – fortune through the invention of bleach in the Industrial Revolution'. The 'albeit vast' is instructive; the wonder being that such a simple product, used in modern households mainly as a disinfectant, could make a family as rich, if not far richer, than three or four centuries of landowning. But the invention of bleach changed everything. Textiles employed more people in Britain than any other manufacturing industry throughout the nineeenth century, and in some years accounted for two thirds of British exports in an era when Britain dominated world trade. A chemical mixture that shortened the bleaching process from months to hours played an essential role in Britain's industrial growth.

After his weaving apprenticeship was over, Charles Tennant began to show signs of commercial and social ambition. He took on a further apprenticeship, this time as a bleacher, and he and a business partner bought a few Paisley bleachfields cheaply. Marriage followed to the daughter of a part owner of an alum factory – alum was an important ingredient in cotton dye. Socially as well as professionally, he had secured his position among the up-and-coming of Scotland's new industrial class. Another partner in his father-in-law's factory was the chemist Charles Macintosh, the raincoat inventor, and he and Tennant became friends and fellow experimenters, members of a small scientific community that had Glasgow University at its centre, and the steam technologist James Watt and the chemist and physicist Joseph Black as its distinguished mentors. By the late eighteenth century, scientists in Sweden and France were experimenting with chlorine as a whitening agent, but its harmful effects on the human body made its industrial use too dangerous to be practical. Then the French chemist Claude Louis Berthollet discovered that the chlorine solution could be made less noxious by adding an alkali. Learning of this, perhaps from James Watt after a visit to Paris, Tennant and Macintosh opened a small factory that produced bleach on the Berthollet principle, passing chlorine gas through an alkaline solution of slaked lime and water. It wasn't a success: the liquid mixture was unstable and cumbersome to transport. Within a year, the two partners had devised an alternative by changing the state of the mixture from liquid to solid. Passing chlorine gas over slaked lime that was damp enough to absorb it, and then drying the lime and crushing it into powder, they made what Tennant called 'bleaching salt'.

A patent was granted in 1799 and within a few years bleaching salt had become an indispensable part of cotton and linen manufacture. A new factory was needed. Tennant chose a two-and-a-half-acre site by the canal in St Rollox, a northern district of Glasgow. Barges brought fuel from the Lanarkshire coalfield and took away bleaching powder to wherever it was wanted. Over the next forty years, the factory grew to forty times its original size and diversified into other chemical processes, making the soda needed for soap production and the vitriol (sulphuric acid) that increasingly went into the manufacture of so many things, including bleach, dyestuffs and fertiliser; so that by the time Charles Tennant died in 1838, St Rollox looked like an industrial San Gimignano. Prints made to commemorate the opening of the first railway to reach Glasgow, which Tennant promoted and helped to finance, show trains of flag-flying carriages steaming neatly to and from a cluster of smoking towers on the horizon. In the foreground, two gentlewomen with a picnic basket sit in a field where sheep graze further off. Close to, a beautiful tree in full leaf represents nature pure and undamaged.

Of course the reality was different: as early as the 1820s the St Rollox factory was prompting bitter complaints from those unlucky enough to live near it. A pall of yellow smoke hung over the factory day and night. 'The smell of the works is at all times very offensive when the wind is north and makes her sick and inclined to vomit,' a complainant's lawyer told an inquiry in 1822. 'Whenever the wind is in the north it pours down upon her. She considers this wholly arises from the manufacture of vitriol – and if Mr Tennant would give that up, she would let him carry on the other thing as he pleased.' Another resident described the damage done to the vegetable crops in local gardens and hedge plantings: 'During the present season several thousand of seedling beeches along with six thousand seedling thorns have been entirely destroyed.' Twenty years later, a cartoon ironically captioned with the words 'St Rollox . . . a Clear Day' showed nothing but a roiling sea of black ink. Tennant's Stalk was built as the solution, but people were quick to doubt its efficacy: winds certainly drove its fumes further away, but on still days the pollution stayed as local as before.

To be outside the works was bad; to be inside them almost insufferable. In 1847, a civil engineer, George Dodd, described Tennant's as 'infernal in appearance as we can well imagine any earthly place to be', with its 'heaps of sulphur, lime, coal and refuse . . . the intense heat of the scores of furnaces . . . the smoke and thick vapours which dim the air . . . the swarthy and heated appearance of the men . . . and the various acids which worry the eyes, and tickle the nose and choke the throat'. But the Tennant family's confidence in the enterprise never weakened. They knew their products were essential to Scotland's prosperity; in evidence to the 1822 inquiry, two mill owners said it would be a 'national calamity' if the St Rollox factory were to close even for a few weeks. And so it went on flaming, smoking and fuming on Glasgow's northern heights. In the 1870s, a Glasgow health inspector could still remark that 'a sparrow didn't dare fly over the works' for fear of losing its life.

But dangerous and nauseous as the fumes might be, they were eventually dissipated in the atmosphere. Soda ash, which the factory began to make in 1816, brought a far more permanent problem. An essential chemical in the glass, textile, soap and paper industries, St Rollox pioneered its manufacture by the Leblanc process, the invention of Nicolas Leblanc, physician to the Duke of Orleans. The process used expensive ingredients – rock salt, limestone, sulphuric acid and coal – and it was tremendously wasteful: every ton of soda made in the factory produced two tons of hazardous waste, high in sulphur content, liable to give off hydrogen sulphide (the gas that smells like rotten eggs) and sometimes to catch fire of its own accord. Eighty tons of it came out of the vats every day, to be dumped on the open ground west of the factory, where it eventually covered a hundred acres and in places reached down eighty feet. It became a hideous grey wasteland: a dystopian park with a dismal water feature, the Pinkston Bog, where seeping groundwater mixed with the alkali, to be drawn off by pumps and course down various sewers and streams to add to the Clyde's pollution.

This was the blighted land I saw from the train, and it need never have grown so large.

In 1872, the company rejected a cheaper, less wasteful and cleaner method of making soda that had been devised by the Belgian chemist and industrialist Ernest Solvay. Nobody understood so at the time, but the rejection of the Solvay process was a blunder that marked the beginning of the Tennants' long – and at first barely perceptible – industrial decline, a downward line on the graph that more or less matched Britain's performance over the same period as it was overtaken as the world's pre-eminent industrial power by the USA and Germany. The Leblanc method couldn't compete on price, and by the 1890s most of the world's soda ash came out of plants using Solvay's alternative, which in Britain had been licensed to Tennant's rivals, Ludwig Mond and John Brunner. The Tennants decided to stick with what they knew rather than risk capital investment in new technology. It was a conservative decision and, like many other aspects of the Tennant story, it exemplified what a century later was to become a conventional explanation of British industrial failure.

What British industrialists lacked was sticking power: in an English culture that viewed industry as an unpleasant intrusion into the rural idyll, they were too easily seduced by transformational ideas of themselves as landed aristocrats and country gentlemen. Show them a peerage, a steam yacht, a foxhound pack, a trout stream, a grouse moor or a golf course, and they went off hallooing in pursuit. A pattern emerged. The early generations made the fortune, the middle generations consolidated it, the later generations spent it: hard work, followed by the intelligent investment of profits, followed by freewheeling pleasure and decay. One or two members of the Tennant family began to understand themselves in this way. *Broken Blood*, a fine study of the family dynasty by a junior member, Simon Blow, has lives-gone-wrong as its theme, and the same melancholy preoccupation haunts Emma Tennant's final book, *Waiting for Princess Margaret*, in which she resents her half-brother Colin Tennant for his narcissism and because, when their father died, he quickly expelled her from rooms she kept in the family home in a dispute over their father's legacy.

4. The scene at Basil's

I met Colin Tennant in 1979 on Mustique, where I went to try and write an overambitious piece in which the leftist movements that were then growing in the Caribbean would be seen through the prism of the wealthy Europeans and North Americans who spent their spare time on Tennant's island. I remember that he wore a wide-brimmed straw hat and what India knows as *kurtha-pajama*, a long white shirt over loose white cotton trousers, and that we talked in a kind of Moghul kiosk that he'd erected near his house on the beach. He was tremendously affable, talking knowledgeably about the island (by now he was only a minority shareholder in the company that owned it) and inviting me to see the Caribbean plantation islands 'as the Middle East of the eighteenth century', with sugar rather than oil as the energy source that the world wanted. There was more talk about oil – its high price, combined with the low price for Caribbean exports such as bananas and bauxite, had lowered living standards on several islands, with social unrest as a consequence. Tennant was unflappable at the prospect of a new order. 'When a stranger walks into the room,' he said, as though the world were a London club, 'you don't turn your back on him or shout rape. You go up and shake him by the hand.'

He showed me the sights. They included the wreck of a French liner, which had been stranded offshore for years and now broke up the waves like a reef; Basil's Beach Bar, a small platform that stuck, pier-like, into the sea; and, from a respectful distance, a view of one or two of the pseudo-classical villas that had been designed by the celebrated English stage designer Oliver Messel. Eventually we reached the group of huts known to a few islanders as 'Tennant's Tenements', which housed the domestic servants who served the villas. Most were temporary migrants from St Vincent, the closest of the larger islands, and their huts were the equivalent of tied cottages: if they lost their jobs, they lost their homes, too, and went back to St Vincent. The huts had nowhere indoors for their occupants to wash. Tennant said they were waiting for showers to be installed – 'But these people are much better off here than they would be in St Vincent,' he said, trying to complicate and soften the simple moralism of an outsider.

That night I went to Basil's Beach Bar. This had taken some negotiation, because Princess Margaret was to be there, too; she was leaving the island the next day, and after the farewell supper party at her villa, Les Jolies Eaux, she wanted to have a more intimate drink with one or two friends. If I went, Tennant said, I mustn't approach her or speak to her.

'You promise?' Tennant had asked, and I did. But it was difficult. Basil's consisted of a small bar on the landward side and a dance floor that projected over the water. The bar stools nearest the entrance were taken by two men who were part of the princess's protection team. Her private secretary, Lord Napier, sat on the next stool towards the sea, beyond which there were a few empty stools and then ones occupied by the princess and her lover, the landscape gardener Roddy Llewellyn. I took a stool between the courtier Napier and Her Royal Highness, closer to him than to her. I asked him if he were by any chance a descendant of the Edinburgh man who invented logarithms (John Napier of Merchiston, 1550–1617, whom we learned about at school), and he smiled and said something like, 'I think I might be.' In fact, as John Napier's son was the 1st Lord Napier and he was the 14th Lord Napier, his connection to logarithms was reasonably direct. But if I'd known more about the Napiers, and asked if he was related to the Napier who had stood in as a temporary Viceroy of India (the 10th Lord) or the Napier who first proposed that the British seize Hong Kong (the 9th Lord), the answer would probably have been just as diffident and final.

The conversation stalled. I looked around in time to see the princess stub out a cigarette, rise from her stool and walk towards the lavatory in the bar's dark backyard, accompanied by a detective who lit her way with a large torch. When she returned, she and Roddy danced alone at the end of the little pier. She was wearing a kaftan; no legs were visible. Roddy wheeled her around like a much-loved piece of furniture, as though she had castors rather than feet. Aware of my sad – and, no doubt to her, irritating – position as a dumb voyeur, I walked back through the darkness to the hotel.

'He is an immensely charming man and Mustique is a testament to his charm . . . the island is a triumph of publicity rather than nature,'

I wrote in the piece, blind to the fact that the person most dazzled by this charm – most in love with the power of it – was Tennant himself.

Vanity was a family trait, with Colin's Uncle Stephen as perhaps its most extreme example. In his family memoir, Simon Blow remembered how he would sit in Stephen's bedroom and listen to him reminisce. 'I think there's no doubt that I do have great beauty,' was a typical statement. 'Have you ever noticed the shape of my nose? If I lie like this you can see the nostrils . . . lovely, aren't they?' V.S. Naipaul lived for a time in a bungalow on Stephen Tennant's Wiltshire estate, and in his memoir-novel *The Enigma of Arrival* writes that his landlord's apparent shyness 'wasn't so much a wish not to be seen as a wish to be applauded on sight, to be recognized on sight as someone stupendous and of interest . . .' Colin's paternal grandmother, Pamela Wyndham, had the same need to be noticed, leaving the dinner table to stand and face the wall if she thought other guests were ignoring her. Her granddaughter, Simon Blow's mother, was no different. Blow remembered how, 'after a children's party [or a wedding] where other mothers were present, we would always be asked, "Who was the most beautiful woman in the room?" . . . The answer, of course, we knew: "You, Mummy."'

5. How to become a baron

During the reign of the second Charles Tennant, the first Charles's grandson, the family began to leach its Presbyterian genes. The second Charles came to be known among his friends and family as 'the Bart' after the baronetcy Gladstone awarded him. In the Tennant story, the Bart is the Sun King, the imaginative investor and share speculator, art collector, country house builder, London society host, Liberal politician and party funder, and, not least, ever-virile patriarch: the father of sixteen children (four of whom died in infancy), the first born in 1850 and the last in 1904, when he was aged eighty and six-years married to his second wife. The Bart made a separate fortune in railway shares when he was still in his twenties; he founded a steel company, invested in Indian goldfields, exploited the world's largest deposits of pyrites in Spain; and by the time of his death in 1906 could count himself the sixth richest man in Europe.

Under him, the family distanced itself from the primary source of its wealth: London and not Glasgow became the family home, and the London office replaced the Glasgow office when it came to the biggest decisions. His sons went to Eton rather than the modest Scottish schools that he and his forebears had attended.

Increasingly, Scotland took on an idealised role as the dynasty's birthplace and, more practically, as a country to return to in summer. Not to Glasgow, but to the great mansion called Glen that the Bart had built in the Scottish Borders, a fantasy of turrets, towers and crow-step gables that emerged among bare hills like a lovely mistake, a chateau in the wrong landscape. It had fifty rooms and a hundred servants, and the estate around it eventually grew to 10,000 acres – an area occupied by grouse moors, sheep pasture, a boating pond, a fishing loch, avenues of mighty North American trees, a school, a post office and handsome villas and cottages for the farmers, labourers, shepherds and gamekeepers who worked the Tennant land.

Glen turned out to be the dynasty's most enduring feature, the scene of its greatest social achievements, the place most associated with the Tennant name. I went to stay at Glen in the winter, which is a month or two ago as I write. The estate describes itself as a 'farm and residential community', but the big house has an apartment converted from the old kitchen quarters that can be rented by the week, and it was there I stayed with my wife and two friends.

The weather was bitterly cold and blustery, with sunshine and blue sky switching suddenly to squalls of sleet and snow. The hills were white – sometimes the gardens, too – and the burn at our front door ran noisily with meltwater, like a constant ripple of applause. Water had always been a notable feature of the place. Luxury had once been, too: one of Sir Charles's granddaughters remembered how money 'seemed to flow in (and out) of Glen as easily as the brown burns flowed down the hillside'. At dinner, Sir Charles liked to boast every pineapple on the table had cost him five pounds to grow. But to judge by the way our central heating was rationed, expenses were watched more carefully now.

Still, ours was a handsome apartment, expensively adapted from its original use as a larder and decorated with not-too-valuable heirlooms, including a wooden box, seven feet long by nine inches wide and fastened with leather straps, which lay propped against the wall. A small metal plate engraved in copperplate indicated that it had been the property of Edward Tennant, 31 Lennox Gardens, London; an old luggage label – ST PANCRAS – suggested it had travelled to Glen in the days when expresses from London ran directly to towns in the Scottish Borders. It was the box he must have used to carry his fishing rods – a heavy box that would have needed manhandling by station porters in and out of luggage vans and a servant to carry it up the two miles of track that led from the house to the fishing loch that had been made by damming the streams at the head of the glen. It was named after him – Loch Eddy – and one morning we walked there, stopping to shelter from snow squalls on the way, to find a dark little lake surrounded by silver birches and evergreens.

A wide-eaved boathouse sat neatly on the shore, with a bench where a fisherman could face the water and smoke a pipe. The sun came out and gave the scene an Alpine touch. It was good to sit here for a moment and consider the little loch that, his children apart, was almost certainly Edward Tennant's greatest creation. Unlike his father, Sir Charles, the Bart, he had a poor head for business – and yet he'd risen further up the slopes of the titled classes to become a baron, a genuine peer of the realm with a seat in the House of Lords, rather than a baronet, an ambiguous ranking that put his father somewhere above a knight but still a commoner. What had caused his elevation? The explanation was a politician's need for money. When, in 1894, Eddy's youngest sister, Margot, became the second wife of Herbert Henry Asquith, then Home Secretary in the Liberal government, Sir Charles endowed her with an income of £5,000 a year (roughly half a million in today's money) and gave the couple a grand house on the borders of Mayfair. But his wife's dowry wasn't enough for Asquith, who had no great private income of his own, so Sir Charles supplemented it with regular lump sums, a habit that Eddy continued after his father's death, just as he went on paying off Margot's frequent debts at the bridge table. When Asquith became prime minister, his financial needs grew. Every year Eddy sent him a cheque. Sometimes Asquith was importunate. 'I find that with illnesses, operations and constant journeyings etc., this has been a very expensive year,' he wrote to Eddy in 1913, shyly continuing: 'I should therefore be greatly obliged if you could anticipate now what you are kindly in the habit of giving me in the spring.'

By this time, Eddy already has his reward. Asquith raised him to the peerage in 1911, when he became the 1st Baron Glenconner (of The Glen in the County of Peebles), honouring the Ayrshire farmstead where his family's good fortune had begun.

Perhaps Eddy sat in this same seat after a morning's fishing and thought of that farmstead, imagining how it might look – nothing suggests he ever went there. There it lay over the hills, thirty miles and three watersheds away across the Southern Uplands: a whitewashed building as simple and picturesque as Robert Burns's cottage; proving, like the poet's birthplace, honoured as a national shrine almost from the moment the poet died, that genius could have the humblest origins.

6. In memoriam

What remains of the Tennants? Other British industrialists of their era are remembered for their philanthropy: Carnegie, Leverhulme, Rowntree, Cadbury. Restrict the names to Scottish textiles alone, and you have the Coats family, the Paisley thread makers, and the Cairds, the Jute kings of Dundee. Even quite modest family enterprises managed to fund a decorative fountain, a public park, a drinking trough for horses. But so far as I could tell, sitting in the cold kitchen at Glen and reading their family history, the Tennants had done none of these.

Before we left Glen, we went to look at the family's memorials in the graveyard of Traquair Kirk, which stands on the edge of the estate. Snow covered the ground, making identification difficult, but at last we found the family plot. There was nothing grand about it, no statuary, nothing that suggested bombast or vanity. It looked uncared for. Eddy's little headstone was broken in half and we needed to scrape moss from Sir Charles's flat tablet before his name could be made out. More scraping revealed a legend on the low boundary wall separating the Tennants from the parish's poorer dead: UNTIL THE DAY BREAK AND SHADOWS FLEE AWAY.

There were fourteen of them in all, from five generations: Sir Charles and his children Eddy and Laura, Eddy's son Christopher and Christopher's son Colin and Colin's son Charles. Uncle Stephen, for whom heather was too purple, lay elsewhere – in Wiltshire – but at home in London I discovered that he had a kind of memorial – it was described as 'a shrine' – in the East End borough of Hackney, which despite its gentrification isn't the kind of place anyone would expect to find Tennants of his generation. One afternoon I walked along the canal to its location, the Viktor Wynd Museum of Curiosities, which lay in the basement of a dark wine bar on Mare Street. A £3 entrance fee – perhaps a senior's discount – allowed me to step down a twisting iron staircase into two rooms that brimmed with a Victorian showman's idea of oddity. Display cases held preserved penises, shrunken heads, Regency cartoons of plump fornicators, two-headed kittens, a hairball from a cow's stomach, models of human viscera, fish skeletons, repellent insects and faeces that had allegedly come from celebrities. A bottle labelled 'Russell Crowe's urine' stood in one display case. Another held items allegedly found in a bedroom of a Sri Lankan club after one, other or all of the Rolling Stones had vacated it: condoms that had turned hard and yellow and an empty packet of Viagra.

A display of Stephen Tennant memorabilia – a reliquary – occupied an ill-lit corner. There were a few framed pictures of him, a photocopy of a review of Philip Hoare's biography headlined 'The Man Who Stayed in Bed' and several of his overripe drawings, including a cover for the novel he never wrote, *Lascar*, subtitled in this version *A Story of the Maritime Boulevard*, showing lusty young mariners stripped to the waist. That was all.

'An idle, silly queen,' wrote Paul Theroux, '[he] was upper class and rich, so people laughed at his jokes and called him marvellous.' It seems a reasonable verdict. But to be remembered in this squalid basement? Whose memory deserves such a fate?

7. Galligu

In my first autumn in Glasgow fifty-seven years ago I met David, who is now my oldest friend. Both of us studied in the evening in the reading room of a grand civic institution, the Mitchell Library (the nineteenth-century bequest of a Mitchell who owned a tobacco business), and when the bell rang for closing time at nine we were among a group that went to a cheap restaurant nearby that sold beer so long as some food – a mutton pie and chips, say – was part of the order. David lived then in a tenement in Cowcaddens, a part of the city that was said to be among the most densely populated districts in Europe. (Glasgow's technological boasts in the nineteenth century – tallest, largest, fastest – had been replaced in the twentieth century by record-breaking social statistics – densest, poorest, sickest – that turned fame into infamy.) It wasn't far from my bedsit, but the ten-minute walk crossed a social boundary. Whereas I paid thirty-five shillings a week for a room in a four-room flat that had a bathroom and kitchen, David shared what Glasgow knew as a room-and-kitchen with his widowed mother and grandmother, who slept together in 'the room', while he had a recess bed in the kitchen. A lavatory just outside the flat's door was shared with their neighbours. Heat came from the kitchen's coal fire. The flat had no bath and no running hot water: the kitchen sink was the only place to wash. More ambitious washing, of clothes as well as flesh, required a walk to the municipal baths and laundry, a walk that David, his mother and grandmother regularly made, conveying the weekly wash in a bogey, a little cart on a four-wheel pram chassis. His mother had lived there all her life – until the 1940s with her two brothers and her father as well as her mother: her parents slept in 'the room' and her brothers in the kitchen, while she made do with a windowless cupboard.

Writing this, what strikes me is how unremarkable David's living arrangements seemed at the time. Until the 1960s, when the tenement clearances began in earnest, the room-and-kitchen and the smaller, one-roomed 'single-end' flat had characterised Glasgow's housing stock. If his father had survived tuberculosis, David might not have lived in one; but it struck few people, least of all David, that it was extraordinary that he did. Glasgow's population multiplied ten times between 1800 and 1900, from 77,000 to 762,000 people, and didn't stop growing until it reached a peak of around 1.1 million in the 1930s. In the first decades of the last century, between 60 and 70 per cent of Glaswegians lived in dwellings comprising only one or two rooms. Tenements that were three, four and five floors high – each floor with four apartments and, at best, only basic sanitation – could charge low rents to low-wage earners: they were a way of piling people high and selling them cheap. Out of their doors and clattering down their gaslit stairs every morning came the thousands of men and women on their way to the factories that had made Glasgow's reputation: iron forges, locomotive workshops, cotton mills, shipyards and chemical works.

In the 1950s, respectable children in such places spent their free time – the hours they weren't asleep or at school or helping to trundle the bogey towards the baths – in much the same way as respectable working-class children did elsewhere in Scotland. They read books and comics, belonged to Wolf Cub packs or the Boys' Brigade, listened to radio comedies, went reluctantly to church. There were also those small adventures known as 'expeditions' in which one or two friends, or even a small gang, would roam across the city, unaccompanied by adults, to find dangerous pleasures in unpromising locales. In this way, David found the alkali wastes that the Tennant factory had left behind, joining other children there to toboggan down the grey slopes on a piece of cardboard that he'd brought along for the purpose. He would reappear at his tenement door as dusty as a sack of flour. He remembered how angry his mother would be. 'Just look at the state of you!' she'd say, begging him never to go there, wherever it was, ever again.

That would have been in the early 1950s, a lifetime ago. After university, David began his long career teaching history in the state schools of city districts and nearby towns, each with their own story of industrial decline. Former pupils speak of him as a fine teacher – inspirational, amusing, vivid in his accounts of unpromising subjects such as the Franco-Prussian War. And, somehow, we never lost touch. So it was that on a damp and windy afternoon last winter we walked together towards the site of his childhood adventures on the wasteland, uncertain of what remained.

In 1883 the government's Alkali Inspectorate published the first official attempt to determine the St Rollox wasteland's composition and extent: 'nearly 100 acres of crude calcium sulphide constituting a vast grey desert, a mass of three million tons in some places 24 metres thick'. In the large chemical factories of Lancashire, which supplied the cotton industry and were old rivals to St Rollox as soda producers, waste of the same kind acquired a name: galligu, a word without any known etymology, perhaps a kind of onomatopoeia coined by the chemical workers who had to dispose of such a viscous, lava-like, rank-smelling mess.

The St Rollox factory closed in the early 1960s. In 1963, a year before its demolition began, an examination of the galligu by analytic chemists established that it dated from the period 1825–95 when the Leblanc process was in full swing, and that time and exposure to oxygen had rendered it a 'relatively inoffensive' mixture of calcium sulphate and calcium carbonate, which had an odour of sulphuretted hydrogen (rotten eggs) and hardened when it was dry. As for the Pinkston Bog, it was now better known by the name generations of children had given it: the Stinky Ocean. 'The liquor in the marsh had an offensive smell,' the analytic chemists concluded, 'but the sulphide content was not excessive. The sludge comprised mainly lime compounds, carbonate, sulphate and sulphide, with a quantity of ferrous sulphide which imparted to it a black colour.'

Glasgow shrank throughout the 1960s and 1970s. Landmarks disappeared. One of the railways through the wasteland closed and its track was torn up, leaving an empty cutting that was filled – and the Stinky Ocean with it – with the debris of the tenements that were being demolished elsewhere. Then, in an act of civic utopianism that now looks like self-hatred, Glasgow drove a motorway from east to west close to the central city, obliterating the mainly Victorian townscape that lay in its path. Churches, second-hand bookshops, snooker halls, the old canal, pubs, warehouses: all of them went. David's tenement, in fact his whole dense district, came down, as if an ants' nest had been trodden flat.

The galligu, however, remained intact. New estimates put its volume at a million cubic metres. Mostly, it was invisible, obscured by layers of topsoil, but its inherent instability made it difficult to build over, and contaminated groundwater still leaked out. In 2016, the city council decided it would make the site a Transformational Regeneration Area, a TRA, and announced plans to develop it as an inner-city suburb of a thousand homes, with a church, school, shops, cycle paths, new roads and bridges, and several thousand bushes and trees. The project, known as the Sighthill TRA, is said to be the largest of its kind in Britain outside London, with a budget of £250 million funded by local and national governments.

David and I walked there via the necropolis – the city's steep hill of the dead, where the first Charles Tennant is buried – and then by negotiating motorway slip roads and dank pedestrian underpasses we at last reached the barriers that guarded the former site of Charles Tennant's great works.

Solving the problem of the galligu – making it safe – has been the work of an environmental consultancy whose technical director, Alan Shepherd, met us at the gate. Essentially, the galligu has been quarantined. First, boreholes established its underground location, and then an encircling trench was dug, 1.6 kilometres long, up to eighteen metres deep and between sixty and ninety centimetres wide. A mixture of concrete and an absorbent clay, bentonite, was poured into the trench and a multiple-layer membrane (clay, textile and plastic) stretched across the land inside the trench's boundaries, an area that was then covered in clean soil to a depth of 2.5 metres to allow foundations to be built and pipework and power cables to be laid without breaching the membrane and making it less waterproof. As Shepherd talked, I imagined it as something like a one-tier wedding cake, with the galligu as the filling inside the icing, and natural bedrock and glacial clay as the cardboard base. At a cost of around £20 million to £30 million, this underground architecture was designed to keep the galligu dry – to seal it from rainwater and halt flows of groundwater, and so prevent the leaching of contaminants and the smell of rotten eggs.

Shepherd and the site manager, Bill Allen, took David and me on a tour of the development. They were helpful, knowledgeable men, keen to oblige our interest in the past, though very little of that past now remained. Bill showed us the roadside verge where he reckoned Tennant's Stalk once stood. Elsewhere we found yellow bricks, some loose, others embedded in the ground, which Bill thought looked like the shattered base of a chimney or an oven. As we were driving to another part of the site, David exclaimed that the road had been the route of the number 16 tram – but the road was a rare and untidy remnant from his childhood, still with a residue of small workshops and warehouses that now specialised in car repairs and food stocks for Indian restaurants. Everything else was transfigured, filled in, smoothed, greened, reimagined and refashioned. Granite kerbstones had been imported from China and laid perfectly by a Portuguese artisan and his assistants; saplings lay in bundles waiting to be planted; the new school was nearly finished; meetings in the new church hall had already drawn representatives from the dozen different communities, including asylum seekers, that had made, or would make, Sighthill their home.

The moral arithmetic of the Industrial Revolution is an impossible computation, a never-ending series of sums. Bleaching powder helped the British textile industry to thrive. Thriving, its factories attracted workers from their rural poverty and settled them in slums. Thriving, its cheap products destroyed the livelihoods of Indian handloom weavers and razed the old economy of Bengal. But if it hadn't thrived, what then? Would the world be more equitable, happier, better clothed, more just?

Judgement of the Tennants – the Tennants in their heyday – is easier. Mustique, Glen and Princess Margaret; trout lochs, Eton and home-grown pineapples: they are all very fine. But there, somewhere under the football pitches, lies the Stinky Ocean. ∎

© LORENZO MARASSO
Another Splash View, 2020

IN BRIGHT LIGHT

Paul Dalla Rosa

The court settled for damages. The damages awarded were over two-point-nine million dollars. The sum was for current and future lost earnings, to be paid by a media conglomerate. They were not Alice's lost earnings, they were a man's, but for one long afternoon her name, among others, trended on Twitter and for weeks afterwards Alice's phone vibrated with phone calls and emails and text messages. Alice changed her number. Then people found the new number. They called her family. They called people she had gone to school with, other actors, crew members on films she had starred in.

For a while Alice had thought she still might be sued. There were conference calls linking one side of the Pacific to the other. Legal counsel in Australia, the States. She took the calls on her patio, where her cell didn't cut out. Risk was discussed. Then it looked like she wouldn't be sued as long she didn't make another statement. But people wanted her to make a statement. Then they tired. The news cycle moved on.

As it happened, Alice rarely left the house, a small, two-bedroom mid-century she owned in Los Feliz, all dark wood, hillside views and glass. She wasn't working. She took in a shelter dog, a black greyhound named Brando. Brando had a scrunched-up face, like a boxer's. He had suffered. Brando ran around the house. Brando peed on the floorboards, the tiles, Alice's bed. His black lips parted, his tongue lolling out. To put his leash on, they wrestled. He bared his teeth. At night, Brando looked like a demon, a jackal. After four days Alice took the greyhound back. She apologised to the shelter staff and, in the hope they would not speak to reporters, donated a sum of money. The shelter staff spoke to reporters.

Alice's friend, an actress who had become an executive producer for a successful show on a streaming service, had an assistant deliver Alice a clear quartz stone. It came in a box and inside the box was a handwritten note. Alice couldn't tell if her friend had written the note or if the assistant had. The note told her the stone could magnify intentions, and just as you could see through the stone to what was behind and in front of it, it would allow you to look through the present and see the same.

Alice didn't do what the note told her to do. She didn't meditate with the stone, but she did sometimes, when anxious, eat an edible, one or a handful of gummies, and hold the quartz as she lay in bed or on top of her bed, and though she didn't think her intentions magnified or gained a sense of clarity, she felt something. Like the glass of an air-conditioned room, the stone was cool to touch, and Alice sensed that outside Los Angeles stretched beyond her windows like an establishing shot, across and over the sycamores and palms, the stucco houses, the lanes of traffic and canyons and valleys, the 45-foot letters in sheet metal and below them the private pools that littered the hills, little dappled points of light.

The hard thing, as Alice saw it, was that something bad had happened to her and it was private and then it wasn't. And now when people thought of her, Alice intuited, they didn't really think of her. They thought about someone else and the things that someone did. Or that she was manipulative, opportunistic, untruthful, a whore. The people who thought these things also said them, online.

The actual event in her mind had long since taken on a kind of filmic shorthand. A meeting in a hotel room, a room of people emptying to two, the declined offer of a drink, an embroidered robe coming undone. Then Alice, alone in a carpeted hallway, stepping aside for housekeeping to pass.

This happened a long time ago, after Alice had appeared in a string of independent features, cheap mumblecore dramas, but before she had been to Cannes, before her fame had waxed and begun to wane, and before she'd starred in the studio-backed period piece which was both critically and commercially panned, but allowed Alice to purchase her house outright.

A decade passed. Alice continued acting. Then the exposé came out and her name was mentioned among others, and Alice didn't know how her name was mentioned, or whether she should say something or not say something, each choice having the potential to be damaging but damaging in different ways. She made a public statement, then she regretted making the public statement, then she regretted regretting the statement.

Alice was in a period between jobs, a period she was intimately familiar with, when it could seem like she might never work again, and then something would come up and she'd be out on location, submerged in bright light, surrounded by technicians or the thin walls of an RV trailer, colour-coded, Post-it-noted scripts spread out before her.

But a role didn't come.

In the now, Alice understood that she needed to do something but what that something was seemed unclear to her, difficult to articulate. Standing on her patio, Alice called her agent, Brett. But Brett didn't answer. It was his assistant. Then Alice realised it wasn't his assistant, but someone else. Alice said, 'Put me through to Brett,' then the voice said, 'Okay,' and then Alice went on hold and then she was taken off hold, and she could hear something, a voice, Brett's, but muffled. Then she was back on hold. Then the first person answered and said, 'Brett's in a meeting,' and she said, 'Who am I speaking to?' and the voice said, 'I'm the intern.' She said, 'I'll leave a message,' but it was too late. The line was dead.

A lice began to take small trips out of the house. Instead of calling her myotherapist out, she got into her car and drove to her myotherapist's office suite. She lay on a white towel and listened to the gurgle of a water diffuser. She was touched and had delicate acupuncture needles placed into her shoulders and neck. She ordered and drank iced coffees sitting at roadside tables. Sometimes Alice noticed a black van idling, and her pulse would quicken, and then the van would keep going and she'd realise it was following someone else, a realisation that sometimes made her feel better and sometimes made her feel worse.

She wandered through luxury department stores. She went to Nordstrom. She ran her hand across bedding as a sales attendant described thread counts. She couldn't tell if the attendant recognised her or not.

Alice asked, 'Does it come in a set?'

She brought the set home, washed the sheets, then let them dry in the sun. It was late in the afternoon. She ate a gummy, not because she was anxious but for the feeling of everything becoming soft around the edges. Then Alice lay on the living-room carpet and watched the light turn technicolour, then fail.

Her mother called from Melbourne. Alice's mother described the things she had to do or things that had happened to Alice's sister, her nieces, the trip her sister was planning, how she'd bought her children travelling clothes, filled out passport forms, visas. And though the call often cut in and out, Alice repeated, 'That's nice. That's nice.'

Alice still spoke with her mother, though they didn't really talk, their lives had diverged so much they no longer shared a frame of reference.

When Alice had only been in LA one year, her parents had flown to visit her. They had visited her apartment, at the time a walk-up off Fountain Avenue Alice rented with three other women. All actresses.

Alice's mother had entered all of the bedrooms and taken the curtains off their rails. She asked Alice where the washing machine was. Alice said she didn't have a washing machine. She went to a laundromat. Alice's mum held the curtains and frowned. Her father pointed outside the window and asked, 'Is that a coyote?' Alice's apartment looked down onto the complex's trash cans. Alice said, 'No, that's just someone's dog.'

Alice's parents didn't want Alice to stay in her apartment while they were there, but with them in their hotel. It had a pool. Her father would sleep on the floor. Alice said no.

Alice took her parents to Hollywood Boulevard to walk the Walk of Fame. She wore large sunglasses. Her parents walked on the stars, the scuffed terrazzo, and read the names aloud. Her father said, 'One day you'll have one,' and Alice said nothing but felt something keenly, something close to pain, because though it was tacky, he had said exactly what it was she wanted.

On the corner of Hollywood and Vine, a woman lay in the centre of the intersection. She was yelling. She screamed. She had her arms above her head and rolled. Cars slowed, honked. They drove around her then away. Alice's parents wanted to help. They began walking onto the road. Alice adjusted her sunglasses. People honked at her parents. It took a moment for Alice to realise she was still only watching.

'Are you listening?' Alice's mother's voice leaked out of the phone.

Alice slept and didn't dream.

'W e're only doing the set cocktails.'

Alice said she didn't drink. Alice felt she was already a little high.

'Like I said, it's set.' Alice thought he was probably an actor. Pouring drinks he was like everyone else. Playing a role.

'Just hand me a Diet Coke.'

The Diet Coke came with a slice of lemon floating in the glass. She took it out with her fingers and walked out onto the deck. She dropped the slice in a garden bed, brought the glass to her lips. She felt light, like air.

Alice wasn't sure whose house it was. She rarely went to parties in LA anymore but had decided to come to this one, coaxed by her friend Frances. Frances was twenty-two, had acted professionally since she was six – the same number of years Alice had – and took college credits online. They had filmed a movie together, years ago, in New York State, going to the same bad karaoke bar after shoots, and still kept in touch. To Alice, the Hollywood Frances inhabited seemed more exciting than the one she did.

The party was in a large house cut into the Brentwood hillside. The house was like being in the future, sleek glass, polished concrete floors. There was a pool and people by the pool but not yet in the pool. Alice stood next to it. She knew Frances wasn't there.

Across the pool, Alice could see an actress who was more famous than she was, someone who could be recognised by first name. People were crowding her. They looked where she looked while never quite looking away from her. They waited to see where her attention was. To talk about what she wanted to talk about. Alice had spent so much time in LA, over a decade, almost two, but this was still something she found difficult to tell, whether the actress was innately magnetic, or if it was just the fame, so much fame that you could see it like a bend in the surrounding light.

Alice looked away. Whenever Alice was at a party with a pool, she remembered an industry party she'd gone to when she first came here. She was twenty-three. The party was hosted by an Australian funding body. It was confusing. There were agents and casting directors all at a hotel, a rooftop bar in the city. There was a pool. A girl, an actress, decided to jump in the pool because she thought it would be funny or that it would show that she was fun, that she could be magnetic. But no one else got in the pool and the girl waited and then got out of the pool and the bar staff gave her a T-shirt and the T-shirt was branded with the name of the hotel. So the woman went to the bathroom and came back, and stood on the rooftop, still damp, wearing the branded T-shirt over her dress. And she stood there, Alice watching, with an expression that was still smiling but also fake, and the girl stayed like that for a while and then she left.

Alice felt like the girl standing wet by the pool, though she was dry and at a different pool and would not go in. She kept thinking people were looking at her, seeing faces in her peripheral vision, but when she turned her head, no one was looking.

Someone said, 'Alice.' A woman was moving towards her. She was a short, middle-aged woman, dressed like a receptionist. She said, 'Frances isn't here yet.' Then she apologised, 'Sorry, I'm Terri. I'm Frances's manager.' Alice looked at her. 'Sometimes we go out together,' Terri said. 'It isn't weird.'

Alice and Terri stood next to each other. Terri looked across the pool and saw the famous woman.

Terri said, 'Is that Kirsten?'

Alice said, 'Yes.'

Terri looked like she wanted to go over. She didn't. She told Alice that Frances had shot a fragrance campaign earlier that day. Alice didn't know when Frances had become famous enough to head a fragrance campaign. Terri said Frances was planning on having a big night. Terri said she had twins, four-year-olds, but tonight there was a sitter so she would also have a big night. Terri repeated 'big night'. Then Terri toasted the sitter. She struck her glass against Alice's but Alice didn't expect it. Alice dropped her glass.

It didn't break. Alice picked up the now empty glass. Some people were looking at her.

Terri waved at someone for another drink, then she narrowed her eyes at Alice. 'We should do a meeting sometime.' Then she said, 'Who's your manager?'

Alice said she didn't have one. Then Terri asked who her agent was. She told her.

'Oh, I don't like Brett,' Terri said. 'No one likes Brett. He isn't classy.'

Alice said, 'Brett's okay.'

'We were on the same flight once,' Terri said. 'Brett and I. This was coming back from Cannes. He was in first so I had to walk past him and he was wearing sunglasses and this cap, this A24 baseball cap. The logo embroidered. You get me. He was wearing an embroidered baseball cap and drinking champagne, and when I went past him he gave me this stupid smile. He's an idiot. Fuck him and that cap.'

Alice stood quietly.

'He does TM.' Alice already knew this. Brett did transcendental meditation. He had spent a large amount of money in an office suite off Santa Monica Boulevard, was given a mantra, and often recommended Alice do the same.

Alice was still quiet.

'I mean,' Terri said, 'he's a fine agent.'

Alice made her way to one of the bathrooms. She felt unsteady. It seemed very important to get to the bathroom. Inside, Alice locked the door then climbed into the bathtub. It was the kind that had been sculpted from a single piece of stone. It was cool on her skin. Alice took out her phone and opened Frances's Instagram.

She watched her latest story. Frances was with a group of people in cowboy hats. Alice didn't know why they were wearing cowboy hats. Alice decided to call Frances. Frances didn't answer so Alice called again. She answered. She said she was close. Alice heard giggling. She heard a man's voice. Alice asked where Frances was. 'I'm still at home. But I'm close. I'm on my way.' Someone giggled again.

Alice got off the phone. She stayed in the bathtub for a while. Occasionally, someone beat their hand against the door. Then she looked at Instagram again. There was a new story. Frances was in a different cowboy hat. Frances held a toy gun.

Alice decided to leave the party. She called a Lyft. But there was a gate and the Lyft wouldn't have the code for the gate, so when Alice left the party she walked down the driveway, passed through the gate, then a second gate she didn't remember passing on the way in. She stood on the road and waited for the car. At times she thought she saw faces in the dark.

The Lyft was air-conditioned. Sitting in the cabin the air was sweet and cool. The driver asked whose house she'd been at, what was the party. Alice said she wasn't sure then put earphones in. She didn't put music on. The car drove.

He didn't take the 405. The car wound through the Hills. It was very dark. The road curved. They passed gated drive after gated drive. Every now and then the trees would open and Alice could see the lights of the city below. They were driving for a long time. Alice slowly felt they were driving in the wrong direction, that they weren't approaching her house but moving somewhere else. The driver speeding out of LA, taking her to the desert, somewhere desolate and vast. She imagined terrible and obscene things. She looked at her phone. She couldn't track the ride's route because, like in so many parts of the Hills, she'd lost signal. She panicked. She put a hand on the door. She wanted to test whether it was locked. She thought she would just open it. A test. She looked in the rear-view mirror and saw the driver's eyes. They met hers. Alice gasped.

The driver pulled over. Alice was home.

In bed, Alice thought she shouldn't take so many edibles.

A lice felt she needed to leave LA.

Her sister invited her on their trip. Her sister and nieces were going to New York. It was her nieces' first time leaving Australia. Alice understood the invitation was a gesture. Alice and her sister rarely spoke. She said yes.

First they would fly from Melbourne to LAX, where Alice would join them, and from there they would board a domestic flight together. Alice would stay with them for the week – she had impulsively upgraded their accommodation to a two-room suite at the Plaza – then return home while they flew on to Disney World, Orlando.

Alice's sister made an itinerary and emailed it to Alice three weeks before they stepped on a plane.

There was news. The week before the trip Brett contacted her. She had been approached for a role.

She met the directors that week, two brothers who worked together, and their casting director in a wood-panelled office in West Hollywood. Her agent had described them as exciting. They wore basketball shoes and were younger than Alice. They hadn't sent her a whole script, only a scene. The scene was a woman confessing that something horrible had been done to her. Alice wasn't sure if it was the kind of role she wanted or, if she took it, what exactly it would mean.

The brothers said they had written the role with someone like her in mind. 'The money people want someone hot right now, but that isn't what it should be. Fuck the money people.' They listed a few other actresses. Alice understood they were actresses who had been written about in exposés. They wanted to test Alice because they were fans of her early work. 'It felt real,' one of the brothers told her, 'like you were close to something.'

'We want that for the role,' the other said. 'She's complicated.'

Alice did what she always did with directors, she repeated them. She said, 'Complicated.'

'Exactly,' the other said.

'What we want to know is whether you can do something. If you can take us to that spot. We don't want you to give us everything, but we want to feel everything.'

'We want next level. Something more interesting than what you've done before.'

Alice thought the performances she had done before were interesting. Alice replied, 'Next level.' Then she did the test, the casting director holding a camcorder, one of the brothers recording with his phone.

She felt what she always felt acting. Even in a test. She felt the relief of being someone else.

For the next few days she didn't hear anything. Then there was a callback, and another callback. One brother called her incredible. The other told her she had what they wanted. She asked her agent, 'Do I need to test again?' Brett said, definitely not. She had the part. Alice asked whether he was telling her she had the part or the directors had said she had the part. Brett replied, 'These are details.'

Alice went to the airport. She passed security. She remembered there were edibles in her bag. She didn't know whether or not she could have edibles in her bag. She took them out and dropped them in a clear plastic bin. She did this discreetly, then she waited.

Her nieces were excited to see her but they were also tired. Her nieces were thirteen and eight years old. When they saw her at their gate they yelled 'Auntie Alice!' Alice mainly saw her nieces in Skype calls. In person was different. Like a very small dog, her younger niece had too much energy in too small a container.

Boarding their flight, the attendant looked at her passport and then said Alice's full name. Some people looked at her. Alice took her passport and walked onto the plane.

Alice's nieces wanted Alice to sit next to them so she sat between them. Alice's sister took a Valium and a strong antihistamine chased with another Valium. She lowered her eye mask. She slept.

Alice's younger niece, Emily, said she wanted to watch *Cars*. Alice used the in-flight entertainment system. She searched. They didn't have *Cars*.

Alice's older niece, Claudia, said they had to watch something else, and Emily whined. She put her hands in the air and sort of flailed them. She made a noise. A person in front of them turned in their seat.

Alice said, 'Both of you shut your eyes,' then slid two Hershey's bars out of her bag. She told them to open their eyes. She gave them the Hershey's bars. Emily was excited by American candy. She hugged her. Claudia left hers on her tray table.

They watched a film in which computer-generated fish danced underwater. It finished so they began another. When she felt Emily get restless, Alice opened her bag and handed her another chocolate bar.

Claudia didn't watch the film but asked about famous people Alice had been in movies with. Then she said names of celebrities and asked if Alice knew them. And Alice said, no, no, no, yes, and Claudia said, that's so cool.

Then Claudia asked if she could take a selfie of them together and Alice said okay. Claudia looked at the photo for a long time and then said it was good.

Emily fell asleep, her breath soft like a small animal's, a trail of chocolate slightly dribbled down her chin. The lights of the cabin dimmed. Claudia put a hand on Alice's shoulder and looked up at her. She said, 'I believe you.' It took a moment for Alice to realise what it was Claudia believed. Alice didn't know what to say so she said, cool.

When Alice got off the flight, she had four missed calls. They were from her agent.

'Okay, they need you to test again,' Brett said. 'They want you, but they want you to test blonde. They need you today or tomorrow.'

Alice didn't make it to the hotel. She took a flight back.

In LA, she wore a bad wig then a worse wig then resorted to a Vons-bought packet dye. The test was delayed one day, then another. The ends of her hair split, frayed. To calm herself, she drove to a dispensary. She stocked up: sativa, indica, hybrids. She drove back home.

Her sister called from the Plaza. Since having children, whenever she was mad, Alice's sister spoke in a whisper. She whispered, then she whispered some more. Alice did what she always did when her family was mad at her. She sent a hamper. Because her sister was in New York, she chose Sahadi's. She rang the store. She wanted to substitute the candied figs. The attendant said eight-year-olds would eat candied figs. Alice said okay and bought the basket.

Alice did the test. She didn't get the part.

Sometimes Alice thought if she looked deep inside of herself, she'd find an animal, something coiled, something snarling. Alone in bed, she looked for it and found nothing there.

A lice lay on the living-room carpet and emailed her agent. In the months since the test, Brett had stopped taking her calls. The actor involved in her case had a film released. A small group of women picketed the premiere. Other than that, no one mentioned it. Alice wrote that she wanted a meeting. The sound of a helicopter, somewhere over the hills, passed, the glass of the house softly shaking. Then Alice wrote a more assertive email. She lay there. Outside, the city was like a piece of impure quartz, everything diffuse, covered in haze. Alice refreshed her emails.

Her niece, Claudia, had emailed to say that she understood why Alice had had to leave them. The email also shared an article from *Teen Vogue* about a certain actress. Claudia didn't think it was right that people thought the actress was crazy but that she agreed with *Teen Vogue* that the situation the actress was in was crazy, the system. *Teen Vogue* wrote that you could change the system. Since the flight, Claudia often sent Alice emails. Other times, she emailed articles that quoted different actresses' Twitter accounts, their tweets and the tweets other celebrities or annoying people on the internet tweeted in response. The conversation. Or Claudia would email that one of her friends had seen a movie Alice was in, and what the friend had thought. Claudia had turned fourteen.

Alice thought the articles were stupid. She didn't read them but wrote back things like 'wow' or 'I'll have to read it later' and then her niece would ask about when she thought it would be okay for her to come to LA and stay with her. To that, Alice didn't reply.

Alice watched television. She rented a film people tweeted about in relation to *Teen Vogue* articles. The movie was about sexual harassment in broadcast news. Alice rented it off Amazon for $14.99. She began to watch it. In the film, a famous actress plays a news anchor, wears prosthetics and speaks in a slightly lower voice. The voice doesn't really have inflections. It is just lower. The performance was nominated for an Academy Award. Watching it, Alice said a few things in a lowered voice. She read her emails to Brett aloud. Alice said, 'I want to have a meeting.' Alice said,

'This is unacceptable.' Alice said, 'My schedule is free.'

She laughed. She was alone in her house. Alice turned off the film.

T he reporter sat in Alice's living room. Alice poured mineral water then put the glasses on coasters. Alice had to concentrate on giving even pours. This was difficult.

She had spent the early afternoon changing from one outfit to another, sometimes swallowing gummies whole. She'd only wanted to take a little, hoping to balance one with the other, one making her go down, and the other up. Then she'd taken some more, recalibrated, and then later, seated in the living room wearing Rag & Bone jeans, thinking 'Rag & Bone jeans', she took a little more.

The reporter was Terri's idea. Terri, Frances's manager, had taken Alice on as a new client, fired Brett, and had a plan for what Alice had to do. Terri had a specific vision. At no point would Alice discuss specific allegations. That was the past.

'I'm excited we're doing this,' the reporter said. The reporter was a woman in black jeans, a sweater. She didn't do *Vanity Fair* profiles, or *Harper's*. She wrote for the *New York Times*. Alice didn't think producers or casting agents read the *New York Times*.

Alice went to say, me too, but stopped herself at 'me'.

There was a knock at the door. Alice opened it. Two men came inside carrying camera equipment, lights. Alice asked what was happening. 'I was told the photographer was Wednesday.'

'Oh, it's not a big deal. He'll take the photo while we talk. It'll be simple. Laid-back.'

The photographer walked up to different walls, looked at them. The photographer asked if they could look at the patio. Alice nodded very slowly. They hadn't waited. They were already outside, then they came back inside. They seemed to move both overly slow and too fast for Alice to follow.

The reporter picked up a book on the coffee table. The reporter asked, 'Is this what you're reading or what you put out for the profile?'

Alice said, 'Sorry?'

'I'm joking.'

'Oh, okay.' Alice wasn't really listening. Alice was trying not to seem high.

'I want to start on something simple,' the reporter said. The reporter began speaking about a court case, a case that hadn't directly involved Alice, but suggested things about a shift in culture. Alice heard the words 'shift in culture'. She wasn't sure what the question was.

'Excuse me,' Alice said. 'I just need a minute.' She got up and walked to the bathroom and shut the door.

She went through the things Terri had told her. 'We'll say you're waiting for the right role but that it needs to be cerebral. Complex. You're reading scripts. You're not just playing anyone. You want something real. You're still waiting for the new Hollywood. The one to come.'

Alice mouthed the words. Her hands felt hot so she washed them. She looked at her hands then she looked at her reflection. She noticed something had happened to her vision. It was like she had been watching a 2D movie that was now 3D.

This seemed funny.

Alice did not want to do the interview, any interview. She didn't want to speak about certain things or represent them on-screen but this was the situation she was in. A situation where the things she wouldn't do became mixed with the things she did. So, Alice decided to do something else.

She opened the bathroom window. She let out a laugh. She stopped herself, then she opened her mouth and laughed quietly. She put a foot up to the window, then an arm. She climbed out. And when she was standing on the patio, she didn't stop. With her bare hands and feet, at the house's lowest point, she pulled herself onto the roof.

She sat down there. What she could see was like the view from her living room, except for the expanse of the sky. It was sunset, the sky a blaze of orange, pink. She thought about the reporter and the photographer and his assistant in her living room. She thought about them sitting in the fading light, sitting there until the room went dark. At some point, they would leave. She thought, 'I'll wait them out.' She giggled. Alice thought she couldn't sit on the roof forever, but she could sit there for a long time. She would do transcendental meditation. She'd see it all and transcend it. She looked out. She could see past the eucalyptus trees of her yard, the cacti, and out past the palms, the entire city.

She said, 'I fucking hate this place.' She laughed. Then she said it again and again. ■

Jesse Darling

In Medias Res

In the middle of this the course of our life, I stopped
& everybody got out of their car.
The crickets roared. Wind farm sliced up blue in chorus,
like syncopated swimmers, all muscle blade & grace.
Young biker soft-shouldered with his leathers off. No ass to speak of
& not much of a face. He whispered of the car on fire ahead,
all reverent, & said:
You can even *see* it, just up *there*.

I walk the broken line like I once walked into the bar,
right down the middle, toes out, & I flashed my brights
at all the girls & boys. Kids, I was gorgeous,
I mean drop dead & I knew it too;
it was all I knew, & not much else. But I was full of speed,
driven by longing for whatever felt like life, or fire,
or a ride out of town into nothing, nothing. & I thought, back then,
that people staring meant desire.

Years pass. & when at last I let the bleach grow out,
I see that my hair has turned grey. An hour or two goes by.
Frosted tips in the camper van tut tuts on the shoulder.
Parched mouth poppies tongue the verge.

Quiet of afternoon except for the rumours, the distant siren,
& breathing gentle fire, the empty car.

When we all drove past
in single file, we marvelled as it burned.
What damage. What elegance.
What happened? What happened here?

COLVILLE

Fergus Thomas

Introduction by Duane Hall

In November 2020, *Granta* editors Rachael Allen and Josie Mitchell had a conversation with Duane Hall, a member of the Confederated Tribes of the Colville Reservation, about *Colville*, a photoessay documenting the bareback horseraces of the community, by British photographer Fergus Thomas. Hall sat with his three-year-old daughter Irene, and talked about racing and how he first met Thomas during the summers of 2015 and 2016.

RACHAEL ALLEN: Could you tell us about the race that's documented in the photos? How does it work? How do people take part?

DUANE HALL: I guess, for the relay races, I don't know how it started. I've never got to the bottom of that, I've never really done the research. But, first of all, it's a lot of intense training. You've got to choose the right horse. You've got to get to know the horse. Train him, pretty much raise him up. And then extensive hours to get to know the horse, get a feel for the horse. As well as your teammates. They've got to be a big part of it. They've got to be there throughout the whole training from start to finish.

And when they get to the races, there's a sense of adrenaline, a kind of animosity, if you will, and a lot of anxious feelings. You can really feel the horses, when you're around them, you can feel their spirit coming to life. They know what they're trained to do, what they're supposed to do. So they're on high alert.

When the race starts, you get tunnel vision. You don't see a lot of stuff. You don't feel a lot of emotions. You just concentrate on what your job is during the race. When the race starts, it's like all bets are off. You don't got no more brothers except for your teammates, because they're the ones who are helping you throughout the race. It seems, in those short minutes it takes to run the relay race, it's every man for himself, and every horse for themselves.

The jockey himself, he has the biggest job. The jockey and the catcher. The jockey has to stay mounted. And the catcher has to make sure the horse doesn't run him over or get away. A loose horse on a track means disqualification. So, if your catcher doesn't catch the horse, or your outholder doesn't keep a hold of the horse, and they get loose, then it's automatic disqualification.

ALLEN: So you have to have a lot of control over something that might not want to be controlled.

HALL: No, you have no control. If the horse is going to make up his mind to take off down the track with you dragging then you're either going to let go or you're going to hang on. The horse, just like a human, they have a mind of their own, they have their own emotions, their own thoughts. And if they decide this is what they're going to do, then all we can do is hang on and pray for the best.

ALLEN: Do you own the horses? Who owns the horses?

HALL: I don't, I don't own any horses. I was fortunate enough to get on a team. One of my good friends, who had been involved in races for some years, one day said, 'Hey, we need a teammate.' And I said, 'Okay, I don't know what I'm doing but I've watched enough, I think I can figure it out.' And so we went on, and it was quite the experience. I just fell in love with it. And actually, a couple of times, I didn't tell no one where I was going. I just packed my bags and headed off to a race, and my family was calling and asking when I was coming for dinner and I said, 'Well, I'm about six hours away so I won't be home for a few days, I'm running these horses.' It's a lot of fun.

ALLEN: Is it dangerous?

HALL: It can be. I don't know anybody who's been severely hurt, knock on wood. They get run over, they get hit by a horse. But not severely hurt, where they can't walk or talk, or even die. I have really great brothers who have won the championship several times. It's amazing to watch them run, they're really good. I like to be behind the scenes when they're doing their stuff, so I can watch and learn, and kind of mimic what they do when I get to be a part of it. So it's all learning, all the time.

JOSIE MITCHELL: What makes a good team?

HALL: A good team? You've got to get a good rider, someone who practices a lot, who grew up around horses. And then you've got to have someone who's got enough bravery or willpower to stand in front of a running horse and grab it while it's running, and stop it. That's another big part. Also a holder who can keep the next horse calm and ready to run the next lap. The outholder is already tired from a lap, and is catching his breath, and doesn't usually try any funny business.

But also you've got to have the right horses, horses that are willing to participate, learn as they're training, run and do their best. Horses are athletes also. They pack the rider. They have to listen to the holder, catcher, you know. It's a big, big picture of what comes down to what you see on the racetrack. It's so many hours of training horses, of practicing, it's like a never-ending cycle, where you have to be a part of your horses' lives as much as they are a part of yours, year-round. I've seen some of my friends drive two hours just to practice for an hour, so it's dedication, lots and lots of dedication. That's what makes a good team.

ALLEN: Do you work with the same horse? Do you race the same horse you work with?

HALL: No, there's three different horses in a relay race, typically. There's a horse race in Emerald Downs that consists of four horses because that's a bigger track. So they divided that up, four horses per race. You start out with your veteran horse. Your veteran horse will, in a way, teach the younger horses, like older brothers teach younger brothers, or dads teach sons, or uncles teach nephews, or cousins teach cousins. It's the same aspect as a human training for a sport. With the horses, they train the same way as a human does. I think, I'm pretty sure, the younger horses watch the older horses and pretty soon they calm down. They get with the program, but it's just lots and lots of practice and training.

ALLEN: What does it feel like when you're in a race?

HALL: It's definitely an adrenaline rush. From the time you start wrapping your horse's legs, when you start getting prepped and ready to go out on track, you're calm, you're taking care of business behind the scenes, getting the horses prepped, getting the teammates ready, or the teammates getting you ready, however it works out. But once you go from the stables, or where your horses are tied up, and start walking out to the track, you get all these thoughts, all these emotions; you get flooded with adrenaline, you're thinking what's the best that could happen, what's going to happen? Your mind has all these questions. But as soon as you hit that track, it's 100 percent business and adrenaline. It's really intense. You can feel your veins on fire from your blood flowing just so fast.

I haven't done drugs, per se. But I drink alcohol quite a bit. The adrenaline rush that you get from the race is like no other high, I believe. I don't know about harder drugs, but once you hit that adrenaline high, I don't think there's anything that can match that. And it seems like it's a rush the whole entire time. And when you leave the track your hands are shaking and you're fidgety, and you're just – whoa, you know.

I never got to experience a whole lot of it. But I grew up around it, watching. But when I did get the chance to try it, I grabbed it and ran with it. I just figured life's too short to miss out on certain things. And watching my brothers grow up doing it, it just made me want to try it more and more. So I actually had to take time off work a few times to just go do it. Just take off.

Nobody really taught me. I just watched and learned, from being around it. I talked to a lot of my friends who did it for a long time, and asked them what it was like. And, they have teammates, they've had them since they were teenagers, or younger, some of them. So they grew up together doing this, and for somebody to step in and take somebody else's place was a rare opportunity. So then I got the chance with Katherine Menthorne's team Umatilla, down in Pendleton, Oregon, which is where Fergus first became a part of the scene.

She'd asked me a year before, or one of her jockeys who's from my hometown said, 'Well, I need a hand, can you help?' And I said, 'Yeah, I'll give it a shot.' And ever since then, every chance I get, I'm jumping on a team. It's a lot of fun, a lot of joking when the teams are walking out. If you do something wrong, the other team, or your own teammates, will correct you, they'll tell you, 'Hey man.' When you mess up, they're your big brother, even though they're younger than you. Some of them are younger than me, but they've been doing it for so much longer than me, they know the ropes so they correct me. It's amazing how close everyone is, until it's time to race.

ALLEN: Did Fergus race, when he was there?

HALL: No, I don't think that he got the chance. But I think that he was more into his photographs over anything. And that was his biggest concern – getting a good picture.

ALLEN: What was it like having him there?

HALL: It was interesting when he first got there. At first, it was kind of like we were babysitters. Katherine brought this 21-year-old young man and handed him to myself and the jockey of the team at that time and said, 'Protect him, take care of him, don't let anything happen to him.' And we were party animals back then, like superbad. And I told Fergus, 'Well, if you like to drink and run around, let's go.' And he survived the first night, so I figured, well, this is going to be a long weekend.

And he was respectful enough that he wouldn't take a picture without asking. And that's what really gained my trust, and other people's trust around him. Because, at first we were like – wait, we're here in Pendleton, Oregon, racing horses at a big Pendleton roundup, partying and running around and whatever. So at first we thought, if he takes the wrong picture, we're going to get in trouble. If he takes the right photo, we're going to get a pat on the back. And he explained a lot to us about what his intentions were so we decided, 'Yeah, go ahead, take as many as you want.'

He was going to stay in Pendleton. But the weekend after the Pendleton roundup, we had our horse races up here at the county fair. And so, myself and Louis Zacherle invited him up, and he stayed the rest of his three-month visa and in that three months, between Louis and me, we brought him out on the mountains and all over to the sites of our reservation. And he just fell in love. He couldn't get enough of it.

I was really surprised the following spring, when he emailed me and asked if he could come over and stay for a spell. So he came over, and I came and picked him up from the bus stop, and he came and stayed at our house. We went out in the woods and I introduced him to everybody I knew. And with that group of people, he found his own little clique who he got to know well enough that he could go to stay at their houses for a time, and take pictures and run around with them, and see other sites that I might not have shown him. And he has a family here, who, when they see him, they open their door and welcome him with open arms. It's pretty amazing to have a guy from anywhere else be that close with everybody around here.

ALLEN: Is he planning to come back over?

HALL: He wants to. But with Covid and stuff, that's the big issue. I think he's trying to save money for whatever he needs. But I've told him that if he ever wants to come back, whenever he can, my door's always open and if he wants to come bad enough, and Covid doesn't prevent that, I told him I'd buy him an airplane ticket. I love the guy. Every time he comes my kids go, 'Oh I remember you, I know who you are.' They just start crawling all over him, it's amazing.

And I am trying to plan a trip over there. When Covid's done, I would love to go over and meet you two, as well as Fergus's family, and his girlfriend, in person. So they can get to meet one of the guys behind the scenes. I think that would be really awesome.

I like traveling. I've worked all over the United States, and I've got to see a lot of beautiful places, and a lot of really rundown sad places, different reservations, and when I saw those places, I'd look at my home and think, I live in paradise compared to some of the places I've seen.

ALLEN: What's your work? What's allowed you to see that?

HALL: Construction. I chase the dollar. Recently, since Irene has been born, I stay home. If I can't find a job here then I make it by. I work on rigs, I do projects here and there, to help us get by.

MITCHELL: Fergus gives this impression of a place that's really special. What do you think makes the Colville Reservation so extraordinary?

HALL: I don't think a reservation is any more special than any other part of the country. It's just what we make of it, because it's all that we have left of the continent. I'm not trying to be *woohoo wahwah*, but our cultural tradition is embedded in us for eternity, and we take that with every generation, and every generation passes it down. Like with our hunting and our fishing. Our land, we try to take care of it in a different way. In a spiritual way that we've been taught from our elders. Passed down.

And I think what makes it so important is we're supposed to be a sovereign reservation, a sovereign people, so we make our own laws and our own rules, and we abide by them outside of the state. But also, I think a lot of people envy us because we get to hunt seven months out of the year, we get to fish all year long, and the non-tribal members around here, they only got a total of twenty days to hunt, so that's what makes everybody think that a reservation is so extraordinary. So when you see relay teams thriving, it's a wonderful sight, and amazing to be able to participate.

MITCHELL: When did you first see the photographs? You were there when they were taken. What was it like to look at the photographs afterwards, and see yourself, and see the things you know so well being represented by this outsider?

HALL: When I see the photographs Fergus took, I feel honored and proud that I got to be a part of that. I got to get him to the destination, and I feel like a picture, a photograph, is a moment in time that might otherwise be overlooked. If someone hadn't captured that moment, you'd never be there again. You can go to the same place, but it won't have the same meaning as the first or the second time. Each time you go somewhere, it has a different meaning, or a different emotion, because it's a different time. And obviously, in time, everyone's life changes, one way or another. But I think with Fergus's photos, I think that it's intriguing to see the different angles and the excitement of him getting out that camera to take any picture at any random place. Everyone says that a picture's worth a thousand words, but you've got to choose the correct words to match the picture.

It's been an amazing experience. The last time that Fergus and I talked, he talked about how much he's matured in the past five years, coming here, taking the photographs, staying with families. And I think that's the same with me. This guy came in, and not only do I have to worry about my family, but this guy from overseas, I've got to make sure he's sent home safe and in one piece. ∎

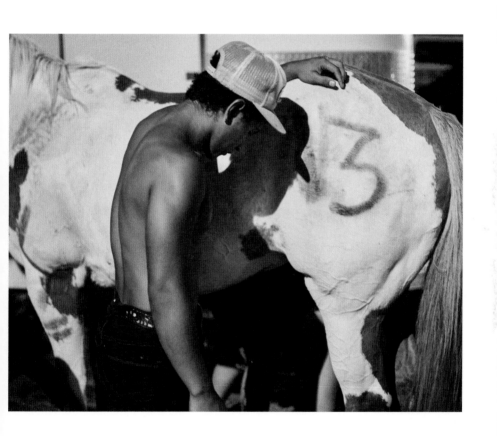

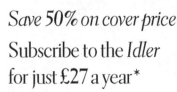

© JENNY MATTHEWS
July 1994, Gisenyi, Rwandan border
A pile of arms taken from Hutu soldiers and civilians as they crossed into Zaire (now the Democratic Republic of the Congo)

WHEN THE CHOLERA CAME

Lindsey Hilsum

In the spring, about two weeks into the coronavirus lockdown, I found myself thinking about cholera. More specifically, about the 1994 epidemic that killed tens of thousands of Rwandans in Goma, in the east of what was then called Zaire. Initially confined to my home, for me the corona pandemic signified absence: no contact with other people, no travel, no access to the sick and dying. In Goma, by contrast, you could not escape the disease. The sick collapsed in the street or on the fields of sharp black volcanic rock that surrounded the town. They died where they fell. Bodies lay unburied, covered by a blanket or wrapped in rush matting. If you weren't careful, you might trip over them.

I remembered walking into a tent erected by one of the aid agencies to see dozens of people sprawled semi-conscious on the ground, their eyes glassy, some drooling thick white saliva, family members sitting next to them, cradling their heads. A lone doctor stood in the middle, crying.

'They're just dying and dying,' she sobbed. 'What can I do?'

The symptoms of cholera are easy to detect: white watery stools and vomit, leading to such a rapid loss of fluids that the eyes begin to sink into the skull and the teeth protrude. Untreated, cholera can cause death in twelve hours, although it's easily cured by rehydration, administered either orally or intravenously. But the doctor had no drips left, or any oral rehydration salts, or – even more critically – a regular supply of clean water. I began to cry too, as we stood together watching people die.

Through my tears, however, I was aware of an uncomfortable reality: the people dying had, not long before, been killing. They were Hutus, Rwanda's majority ethnic group. That April, following the shooting down of a plane carrying the Rwandan president, also a Hutu, their leaders had instructed them to kill their neighbours from the minority Tutsi ethnic group. Lawyers do not accept the idea of a collective crime, but a large proportion of the Hutu population, both men and women, played some part in the genocide, even if only by failing to protect the victims, or turning a blind eye to the killing. In villages and towns across Rwanda, the ideology of 'Hutu Power' – code for exterminating the Tutsis – took hold, and people who had never committed crimes before were mobilised to murder. I had seen something of the genocide myself, as I had been living in the Rwandan capital, Kigali, when it started. Watching cholera take hold in Goma, I was assailed by the violent images I had seen a few weeks earlier: truckloads of people slashed by machetes or beaten with nail-studded clubs arriving at hospital, drunken men armed with broken beer bottles waving me through roadblocks, flies buzzing over four women with their throats slit outside a clinic.

The Hutus in Goma were generally referred to as refugees, but were they in fact fugitives?

An army of Tutsi exiles, the Rwandan Patriotic Front (RPF), had entered Rwanda from neighbouring countries and vanquished the Hutu army and death squads that had spearheaded the slaughter. Defeated, and fearing revenge killings, the Hutu leaders ordered their people to leave the places where they had committed acts of mass murder and follow them across the border into Zaire. How many of the people who were now dying were soldiers who had thrown off their uniforms? Or members of the notorious militia, the Interahamwe? Or *bourgmestres*, village mayors, who had orchestrated genocide in the areas they governed? Or were they just obedient souls who had followed orders, wielding agricultural implements as weapons? Now that cholera had struck, they were in the liminal and unrecognised category of both perpetrator and victim.

It was hard not to wonder if the disease was a kind of divine retribution – collective punishment for a collective crime. When this unmodern thought drifted across my mind I tried to dismiss it. It was not, after all, how I looked at the world. But it wouldn't go away.

There were a lot of large round numbers in those days. It was said that 'a million' people had been killed in the genocide. Similarly, it was said that on 14 July, 'a million' people were queueing to cross the *petite barrière* between the Rwandan town of Gisenyi on one side and Goma, in Zaire, on the other. When I arrived two days later, hundreds of thousands of people were still surging through. Some of the women wore kitenge, the brightly coloured cloth Rwandan women use as a wrap, but many others were in rags and barefoot. Normally you would expect noise from such a huge crowd but these people moved silently, pushing *chukudus*, low long-bodied bicycles with wooden wheels, laden with clothes and aluminium cooking pots. At first the Zairean border guards had attempted to disarm the Hutus; mountains of machetes and hoes and smaller piles of AK-47s and other weapons lay next to the border post. But the guards soon gave up trying to seize weapons, let alone slow or stop the influx.

Goma was a small town then, built by Belgian colonialists on the northern shore of Lake Kivu, in the shadow of a volcanic mountain range that included the Virunga National Park, famous for its mountain gorillas. The jagged black rock that covers the land around Goma is hardened lava from centuries of eruptions. The lava lake in the most active volcano, Nyiragongo, is among the largest in the world. Aerial views show an almost perfect circle of thick, turbulent, boiling liquid with steam rising from the sides. In Rwandan mythology, Nyiragongo consumes the souls of the damned in its fiery cauldron. The day before the refugees started to arrive, the volcano had belched, sending plumes of hissing steam into the atmosphere, a reminder of Nyiragongo's physical and mystical power.

If you turned left after crossing the border, you soon found yourself in the town's fancy district where European coffee farmers, business people and Zairean government officials lived in lakeside villas. Any glory had long since passed – the modest colonial-style low-rises were gently crumbling into disrepair – but despite regular power cuts and water shortages the inhabitants still demanded certain standards of their neighbours. Refugees who tried to set up camp there, disturbing the view of the lake, were swiftly shooed away. Most of the Rwandans plodded straight up the single main street with its dilapidated shopfronts, whitewashed walls grown mouldy in the tropical humidity, past street pedlars selling chewing gum and single cigarettes. They moved en masse towards the traffic circle, from which they could head north towards the airport or out into the bush. Neither of these options was tempting. So hard was the rock, it was impossible to knock in a stake or a stick, or anything from which you could hang a piece of cloth for a shelter from the beating sun. In those first few days, many refugees just slept by the border or in town at the side of the road.

I made notes in a slim school exercise book that I had bought in Kigali. During lockdown, I dug it out of the box where it has remained, unread, for the past quarter-century. The faded blue cover is still smeared with mud. My notes start in almost full sentences.

Just by border one man dead amongst piles of belongings. Another lay a few yards away, next to a naked baby and a man in military uniform. An old ragged man in a woolly hat was going through the belongings, searching the pockets of an abandoned coat.

After that, I jotted down fragments of observation and interview, in English and French.

Piles of machetes and hoes.
'Il y a des bandits.'
Little girl in dirty kitenge, tears on her cheeks.
'I don't think I will find my children again.'

3 heaps of weapons at the traffic circle.

Opposite bodies – 5 children sitting alone and hopeless. Silent. Little girl, eyes closed, thin purple cardigan. Bundle of red cloth – another child. 100 yds of weapons.

Mountains of G3s, Belgian, SA and Chinese. Machine guns. Large automatic. Machine mounted, 2 baby goats sleeping underneath.

My memories are fragmented too; piecing them together was my task during the weeks of coronavirus isolation.

One of the key quests in epidemiology is to find Patient Zero, the first person to contract a disease. In the 1854 cholera outbreak in London it was the baby daughter of Sarah and Thomas Lewis. The London epidemic became famous because it led the physician John Snow to map the incidence of the disease. At the time, it was believed that cholera was spread by 'miasma', foul-smelling airborne particles, but Snow's map showed that the epidemic centred on the well and water pump in Broad Street, just next to a leaking cesspool where days before Mr and Mrs Lewis had cast their sick daughter's soiled nappy. Snow saw the connection, and became convinced that cholera was waterborne, a conclusion that was backed up by the Italian scientist Filippo Pacini, who, the same year, looked through a microscope and saw a comma-shaped bacillus in the intestines of patients who had died of cholera in Florence. Three decades went by before this understanding of cholera's source and method of transmission was accepted, by which time both Snow and Pacini were dead.

In the Goma epidemic, 140 years later, the name of Patient Zero is lost, if it was ever known. Records say that a team from Médecins Sans Frontières found the first suspected case on 18 July, four days after the Rwandans started to cross the border. It was confirmed on the 20th. All that the Rwandan refugees knew was that some of their number began to fall sick in town, and others in the fields of black rock outside the city where the Zairean authorities had told them to set up camp. The ground was too hard to dig wells and the tankers could not deliver enough water. Aid agencies had prepared for 50,000

Rwandans crossing the border, not upwards of a million. There was only one solution: the women had to collect water from Lake Kivu. Mugunga and Munigi camps were only five kilometres from the lakeshore, but Kibumba and Katale were more than twenty-five kilometres away. Still, the women walked as far as they needed, each of them carrying three plastic jerrycans, one on her head and one in each hand. They were, of course, unaware of the tiny, comma-shaped bacillus *Vibrio cholerae* lurking in the shallows, or that the disease it carried was endemic in the area. And even if they had been, what choice did they have?

In poor countries, conflict always brings hunger, disease and hardship in its wake. People die unseen and uncounted, because the hospitals no longer function, or because the vaccination programme has collapsed, or because malnutrition renders them susceptible to tuberculosis or malaria. Deaths from bombs and bullets attract more attention because they're spectacular. But this time, it was the other way around. The genocide had been largely invisible to outsiders – a million murders were concealed among the quiet folds of green hills that enclose the villages of Rwanda. But the cholera that killed the Hutus in Goma was very spectacular indeed. The disease struck in full view of thousands of onlookers – millions if you count the TV viewers.

That was because most journalists had woken up late to the genocide in Rwanda. Distracted by the first democratic elections in South Africa, and unsure what was really going on in this small, far-off country of which they knew little, editors hesitated. Also it was dangerous. By mid-July, more than three months on, realising their mistake but having missed the worst of the killing, editors sent reporters to Goma instead. A TV executive I interviewed later told me he saw the cholera epidemic as 'such a straightforward story – a humanitarian tragedy unfolding daily'. It wasn't straightforward at all, of course. He saw a poor, downtrodden mass of Black People dying of disease and being saved by White People – a version of reality that chimed with his expectations. Others saw a band of genocidal killers protected by a bunch of ignorant do-gooders. The 'straightforward story' version prevailed, at least initially. Pictures were broadcast, money was raised, and more aid workers and journalists landed at Goma's airport, where the runway started to crack under the weight of so many aircraft. Bill Clinton, then US president, who had declined to intervene to stop the genocide, described the cholera around Goma as 'the world's worst humanitaran crisis for a generation', and ordered a large relief effort led by the military. Having failed to save Rwandans who were being murdered, the impetus was to help those who were dying of disease. The fact that these were the wrong Rwandans, the perpetrators rather than the victims of genocide, got lost in the rush.

E very morning aid agency press officers held a briefing full of figures: in my Rwandan child's school exercise book I noted numbers of cases suspected or confirmed, tonnes of supplies needed and litres of water being trucked, and quoted the admissions that they couldn't cope.

'We need one plane every minute bringing in saline solution.'

'Those camps are like hell on earth – volcanic rock. Even if walk in shoes it's painful.'

'There's bubonic plague further north.'

'There are queues hundreds of metres long for water.'

'We're feeling more and more defeated and desperate.'

After the briefing, I would drive with other journalists out to the camps, where people were building flimsy shacks of grass and bright blue plastic sheeting bearing the legend of the UN refugee agency, UNHCR. We grew used to picking our way through bodies. The smell of corpses and faeces was at times overpowering. Until the aid agencies brought in mechanical diggers that could penetrate the rock to carve out latrines, the refugees relieved themselves in the bushes or at the edges of the camps. Flies lighted on the faeces and then on children's lips and noses as they played in the dirt. Everything was filthy, enabling the disease to spread inexorably through the population.

In the midst of such horror, people talked about the humble lives they had left behind as some kind of rural idyll, a prelapsarian existence interrupted not by the genocide but by the arrival of the RPF – the Inkotanyi or 'fierce warriors' – whom they blamed for all their misfortune. Despite the appalling conditions in which they found themselves, they were clear that no families would go back to Rwanda of their own accord, only if their leaders told them that everyone should return.

'As a farmer, compared to others I could say I was rich because nothing was missing in my family – I grew coffee and potatoes, I had cows. But now I have nothing.'

'I had almost 400kg of coffee each season. It was quite enough for me to buy things I couldn't grow like clothes, soap, salt and hoes.'

'I had two radios but they were stolen by RPF soldiers.'

'My parents used to tell me that we would be killed in this war by Inkotanyi. When they talk about Inkotanyi, it means people who kill.'

One day I went to Munigi, where I attempted to interview people as they sat next to the corpses of their relatives lying uncollected on the rock. At the back of a medical tent, where bags of saline solution were suspended from what looked like a washing line, I came across Thérèse Mukaukuranga, who was holding a drip for her husband, Niyitanga. She refused to accept that he had the symptoms of cholera. 'He's been very sick from tiredness since we fled our home,' she said. 'Then he got dysentery.' Dysentery can be fatal like cholera, but to her it sounded less desperate. Thérèse was a plump woman, wrapped in a yellow-and-black kitenge, still looking like the middle-class urban professional that she was, very different from the peasant farmers who made up the majority of those around her. We chatted in French about their life back in Kigali, where she and her husband had been civil servants. *'Nous avons travaillé si dur,'* she told me. 'We worked so hard. We had bought a house and a car.' Thérèse said life had been good before the war and she shrugged off all mention of genocide. According to her, it never happened – it was the Tutsi RPF that had attacked the Hutus. I knew that it was possible, even likely, that she and her husband had participated in one way or another – they worked for the government that had ordered the killings, and had left the country as commanded. It was hard to know what to do with that thought as we watched her husband gradually expire under a relentless sun, so I put it in the growing category of things that were too difficult to contemplate.

The next day I returned to find her still there, her husband again weaker. She was worried about Achille, her youngest son, who was also showing symptoms, and unsure of the whereabouts of her six other children, who had to fend for themselves as she would not leave her husband's side. We were surrounded by the dead and dying. People elbowed each other aside to get a bit of shade, or a slightly more comfortable rock on which their relative could breathe their last. No one else was talking. It was as if, having killed together, and fled together, they now realised that each would die alone, their closest family members reduced to spectators. The following day, Thérèse was squatting by Niyitanga's side as his eyes rolled upwards and his breath came in short gasps. 'I know now that he will die,' she said, quietly. 'What will I do?' By this point my status as voyeur was weighing heavily on me and I apologised for returning every day to interview her when her situation was so desperate. 'But I like it when you come,' she said. 'I have no one else to talk to.'

The next day, she was gone.

My encounters with Thérèse stay with me more than the dozens of others I had in those weeks partly, I suppose, because she was middle class and spoke French so it was easy for us to talk. But it's also because she was, in Rwandan terms, one of the mighty who had fallen. Her descent from civil servant to refugee, from the denial of her husband's illness to acceptance, had been precipitous and must have felt unfathomable. Accustomed to having a large family around her, now she was grateful for the opportunity to talk to a stranger. I don't think she thought I could help her – my daily return with no solution to her problems was evidence of that. As she lost track of her children and watched her husband fade away, she was alone in a way she had never been before – neither family, nor community, or country could help her. Collective crime had given way to collective tragedy and, eventually, unimaginable loneliness.

I never asked Thérèse or any of the other Hutus whether they thought cholera was a punishment, because they denied that they had done anything wrong. They were more likely to believe that the disease was a curse visited on them by their enemy, the Tutsis, whom their leaders had demonised and they had been instructed to kill. In traditional Rwandan culture, hunger, individual sickness and plagues may be caused by *abazimu*, the unquiet spirits of the dead who often communicate through people's dreams. Those spirits would not have stopped at the border. A century earlier, Christian missionaries arriving in the country brought modern medicine and their own religious ideology. According to records of the White Fathers, a Roman Catholic society of priests and brothers, Rwandans sometimes converted because they thought baptism might protect them from dysentery. The European understanding of the supernatural, however, was regarded as less than satisfactory. Modern medicine might provide a cure, but the missionaries' dismissive explanation that, if medicine failed, death was 'the will of God' seemed inadequate. At least diviners and mediums could suggest what might be angering the spirits and what rituals might appease them. By the 1990s, the vast majority of Rwandans were Christians – Catholics, Protestants, evangelicals and a growing number of small sects such as Seventh-Day Adventists. But Mount Nyiragongo, their traditional embodiment of hell, cast its shadow across the camps, and the refugees must have been only too aware that they were dying on the lava that flowed from its belly.

No one had time to count the dead. The World Health Organization estimated after several studies that some 50,000 people died in Goma in that period, 23,800 of them from cholera. People were dying of malnutrition, exhaustion and dysentery as well. A widely respected study funded by the Danish government put cholera deaths at 30,000. Epidemiologists say that only one-tenth of cholera cases show symptoms, so in late July the entire refugee population was most likely infected, and the death rate was exceptionally high because initially the disease spread far more quickly than the aid agencies' ability to treat the sick.

The refugees began to wrap their dead in rush-matting shrouds and carry them to the sides of the camps, where they neatly lined the edge of the road like pale kerbstones. Kevin Noone, a former accountant working for the small Irish aid agency GOAL, hired as many lorries as he could find and started to collect bodies. In his jeans and T-shirt, with no protective gear, he stood on the back of the trucks and hauled bodies, risking cholera himself. The Goma Boy Scouts – some of whom were in their fifties – joined in as volunteers. One reason for the confusion over the death toll was that the aid agencies paid for transportation by the body, so the truck owners inflated the numbers they had carried. After a few days the French military took charge. They threw most of the dead into mass graves they had created by dynamiting the rock some way from the camps. I watched dump trucks tipping bodies into giant trenches filled with quicklime, sending up clouds of white powder which hung in the air before settling like snow on the death pits. A quarter of a century on, when I close my eyes I can still see those uncounted, lifeless, anonymous bodies. No one talked about identifying the dead, let alone funerals or mourning rituals.

Heavy equipment was flown in to drill latrines, and aid agencies installed pumps and water purification units to make the lake water safe to drink. Such interventions were useful; others less so. On the back of the TV coverage, dozens of small organisations around the world raised money to send out staff and supplies with little regard for what was required. The airport clogged up with stuff no one needed: a charity based in Connecticut flew in 10,000 cases of Gatorade – a fizzy drink used by athletes. A photographer friend was near the Katale camp when she heard the roar of aircraft. Three US military Hercules transport planes flew low and dropped parcels into a banana plantation. Local people rushed over to examine the contents: used clothing, Gruyère cheese (marked 'Perishable – Needs Refrigeration'), ski mittens, biscuits (labelled 'Do Not Drop'), chocolate and flour.

United Nations staff sat in sweltering makeshift offices in Goma, trying to coordinate a hundred disparate organisations from all over Europe and the USA. The cholera epidemic in Goma became emblematic of how TV pictures will spur viewers to give money, pulling in aid agencies who may do more harm than good, prioritising the photogenic over the essential. Latrine slabs and drilling equipment do not make as compelling a story as hungry children. Competing aid agencies stuck decals onto every tiny piece of equipment and even onto the lamp posts in Goma. It looked as if the town was hosting some kind of manic election.

Operation Blessing, a department within Pat Robertson's Christian Broadcasting Network, flew in doctors who had responded to a call on the televangelist's daily TV show *The 700 Club*. Most of them had never been to Africa before and each one only came for a two-week stint – just enough time to work out what to do. A reporter friend noticed someone from Operation Blessing running beside a stretcher carrying a dying cholera patient, reading the Bible out loud. 'Operation Blessing tried to cure cholera with the laying on of hands,' said Joel Boutroue, the representative for the UNHCR. 'They are nutcases.' Robertson flew to Zaire with his own TV crew filming him among the ragged children in the camps. 'Call 1-800-759-0700,' he said on his show when he returned to Virginia. 'We could take care of 400- or 500,000 people with one planeload of medicine.' According to his project manager, they did not bring in the intravenous fluids needed but 'enough Tylenol to supply all of Zaire' – in other words, over-the-counter pain medicine. Three years later, the *Virginian-Pilot*, Robertson's local newspaper, revealed that the airstrip he claimed to have cut through the bush so his aid planes could land near the Goma camps had, in fact, been built 800 miles away, near the border with Angola, where he had a diamond concession.

Much of this we only found out later. It was before mobile phones and the internet: we reported simply by finding people and asking them questions. As a freelancer with little money, I took up an offer to stay in a villa with a group of American reporters who were paying guests of a Swiss couple who managed a coffee plantation. Every morning, the wife made us sandwiches, as if we were children going to school. At the camps, children hunted for food or wandered like lost souls looking for their parents.

Little girl sitting on the ground holding umbrella above her, cradling a baby in her arms. She starts to cry because the baby died.

5 children sitting alone and hopeless, silent.

Little boy – triangular face of death.

3 children, lost on Wednesday.

'My parents left me somewhere on the road. I have brothers and sisters. I don't know where they are. When my parents left me, somebody came to help but I don't know who.'

Yandereye, 10 year old girl. Was with parents yesterday night and was separated. 'I am afraid.'

One day, I was driving north with a colleague when we spotted two little girls sitting at the side of the road. They must have been about two and four, and appeared to have been abandoned. Neither had shoes, and their clothes were torn and filthy. They looked blankly ahead when I asked their names. We put them in the car and took them to the nearest tent for what the aid agencies called 'unaccompanied children'. Was it the right thing to do? Had they really been discarded? Were their parents dead? Or had they just left them briefly while looking for food? After a couple of weeks the UN asked aid agencies to stop setting up 'unaccompanied' projects. Parents had begun to abandon their children so that the foreigners would pick them up and feed them, or even take them for adoption in another country. The International Committee for the Red Cross had a centralised system for reuniting divided families, and was the best organisation to deal with lost children, but small aid agency fundraisers knew that pictures of helpless infants would raise money. After a few weeks, most of the fly-by-night aid workers went home, convinced of the virtue of their questionable actions.

After about ten days I heard that a Rwandan reporter I had known from Kigali was in Goma. He was not a person I particularly liked, but I felt obliged to see him because of our previous connection. It was not surprising that he had left Rwanda with the remnants of the Hutu Power government – several people had told me that he was not the neutral voice I had initially thought when I met him before the genocide. He sympathised with the ideology behind it. I made my reluctant way along a rutted dirt road to a cramped room with a cement floor that he had rented for himself and his family on the outskirts of town. Whereas previously he had struck me as arrogant, now he seemed anxious, on the edge of desperation. He needed work, he said, or his family might end up in the camps. He didn't have enough cash to pay the rent. I offered to chase up money he said he was owed but demurred when he suggested I employ him as a 'fixer', a local translator. I didn't trust him. The following day another reporter asked if I would recommend him and I said no.

I can't remember who gave me the news that he was dead but my notes tell the story as reported to me.

Mercredi. He left house in the morning with colleagues. Went to get coffee at Hotel Jambo. Two hours later began to suffer. Went home to bed. Got worse during day and night. Tk to hospital jeudi soir. Gave him treatment. He suffered too much. Started having problems breathing. Died vendredi matin 9am.

I listed the ages of his eight children including *5ans – perdu sur la route.* I don't know if *perdu* means the child had got lost or died. His widow wanted to start a small shop but she had no money, not even enough for a funeral.

I had grown used to death, but this was different, not simply because I knew him but because I believed that it was my fault. If I had employed him, or recommended him, then maybe he wouldn't have contracted the disease. My journalistic principles, which I regarded as a form of virtue, had condemned him to death, and his family to poverty. Finding a few hundred dollars for his widow did little to assuage my sense of guilt. I could not escape from the feeling that I, and the values that I saw as pure in my pursuit of some higher ideal of truth, were implicated. I had allowed myself to wonder if the cholera was a divine punishment, and now I worried that the man's spirit would haunt and punish me.

A s the cholera subsided, it became clear that what looked like chaos concealed an underlying order: each camp replicated the social hierachy that had enabled the efficient prosecution of genocide back in Rwanda. For a while, people had lost track of their relatives but in the end villages regrouped, down to the smallest administrative unit, the ten-household *cellule*. The *bourgmestres* who had organised neighbourhood death squads were now deciding who got food rations. I started to look for well-known architects of the genocide and, sure enough, there they were. I found General Augustin Bizimungu, chief of staff of the army that had led the killings – who was later condemned by the International Criminal Tribunal for Rwanda to thirty years' imprisonment – in a villa in town under the protection of the French military. (The French saved some Tutsis while nonetheless protecting key members of the Hutu Power government.) Bizimungu told me, 'The UNHCR wants us to take off our uniforms and be like civilians. We can do that and go to the camps, and then be recalled whenever we want.' In the months that followed I found half a dozen mid-ranking and senior *génocidaires* working for aid agencies around Goma and Bukavu, further south. They rented houses in town and drove to and from the camps every day, maintaining control over the population and making sure that no one returned to Rwanda without permission.

The cholera epidemic turned out to be just the start of a lengthy cycle of violence and death in eastern Zaire. The camps became bases from which armed groups mounted raids into Rwanda. In one camp I found a Rwandan child's schoolbook just like my own. It contained diagrams demonstrating how to set a charge and plant a landmine, alongside a history of Rwanda according to the Hutu Power myths that saw the Tutsis as *inyenzi*, or cockroaches, needing to be crushed. These were the lessons the refugees were learning after dark when the foreigners had left the camps. Rwanda's Tutsi-led government responded by taking control of the whole area. They orchestrated the toppling of the Zairean regime and installed a new leader who was sympathetic to their cause. The country got a new name: the Democratic Republic of the Congo.

Some refugees were forced back to Rwanda, where many were killed. Others fled further into the bush. The RPF's war of revenge for the genocide was waged not at home in Rwanda but over the border in the DRC. A decade of conflict pulled in all the neighbouring countries and others besides. Some 5.4 million people died, mainly from disease and hunger. Large wars begat small ones, some of which continue to this day. Very few of those who survived the Goma cholera outbreak in 1994 can be alive now.

The medical anthropologist Yuko Otake has explored the Kinyarwanda word *ibikomere*, which translates as 'wounded feelings'. She writes that these may include 'sadness, depression, hopelessness, anxiety, fear, anger and mistrust'. But when she interviewed Rwandans in 2015, Otake noted that 'the most common *ibikomere* were feelings of social isolation and grief – i.e. isolation, loneliness and helplessness, due to the loss of family members'. In the mid-1990s, the whole nation was suffering from *ibikomere*, Hutus and Tutsis alike. The spirits of the dead may cause hallucinations and nightmares, especially if their bodies have not been properly buried. In the years since, the victims of genocide have held many ceremonies to commemorate their dead, but those who lost family members to the cholera or to the wars in the DRC have not been able to mourn in the proper way. The Rwandan government does not acknowledge that its forces killed Hutus after the genocide, so the families of the victims are condemned to silence. The cholera has retreated into history, but the ghosts of those whose anonymous bones lie in the mass graves beneath the black rock may still haunt their descendants.

At 8.30 on the morning of 17 January 2002, a fissure opened on the southern side of Mount Nyiragongo. The air began to smell of sulphur. Vast streams of red-hot molten lava cascaded down the mountainside and covered the land where the camps had been. A kilometre-wide, unstoppable burning snake flowed across the airport runway and continued south into Goma. The town had grown much bigger, swollen by the aid industry and a new interest in minerals like tin and coltan. Hundreds of thousands of Goma residents fled down the street where the mass of Rwandan refugees had moved in the opposite direction eight years earlier. Houses were set ablaze, a petrol station exploded and about a quarter of the town was covered in a two-metre-thick layer of hot, black molten rock. As dusk fell, the lava reached Lake Kivu, sending vast hissing geysers of steam into the air and raising fears that the lake itself might explode. The spirits of Nyiragongo, it seemed, were not content with consuming the souls of the damned, but had risen from their smouldering cauldron to engulf the land where Rwanda's Hutus had fled for refuge and found disease and war instead. ■

Vidyan Ravinthiran as a child, with his family, in Sri Lanka
Courtesy of the author

VICTIM AND ACCUSED

Vidyan Ravinthiran

In Sri Lanka – this was in 2017 – between a golden temple and a shop selling car seats, we found a steel-roofed shack, with, strung across the entrance and the makeshift walls, countless laminated photographs of missing people. Youths. Most male, but there were also women and children looking as young as ten. A teenager stared intensely at the lens, a waterfall of black, wild hair obscuring her left, bared shoulder. The Tamil text at the bottom of each image gave the name and contact details of their family; the posters jostled for room and some were fastened to the corrugated roof.

We entered that space of women – Tamil women – in the shade. Most had grey in their hair, even those lying on the bare, lumpy ground. As soon as we entered, they rose and arranged a circle of chairs, with the expeditiousness of an army unit or a team of cheerleaders. Following the war, their people had never (been) returned. The government said the army and navy would release records, so families would know at last if their children had survived. This hadn't happened.

A vociferous woman (her face stern, with protrusive cheekbones) handed me a sweat-stained sheet of A4. She'd Photoshopped together images of a family – father, mother, two children – and the effect was telling, as if these people never occupied the same space at the same time, but were always destined to separate (the ink had run too, the blacks were green). All of them were likely dead: I saw it in her eyes. She wore a blue sari, tied her silver hair back in a hard bun, and announced: 'We want our children returned to us in the same state they were in when they disappeared.' Which meant she was at war not only with the government but with time itself.

Leaving, I was handed a photograph of a girl who had been 'taken' when she was eighteen. What did this mean, exactly? She could have been kidnapped off the street by the Tigers, and made one of them (there were all-female units, and indeed the Liberation Tigers of Tamil Eelam (LTTE) recruited young people by boasting of gender equality), before dying in battle, perhaps blowing herself up; or she might have been – though innocent – detained by the government and tortured to the point of death, or still incarcerated to this day. Was she sent, perhaps, to one of the camps where Tamils remain political prisoners, with no access to legal representation? Did she find asylum abroad, or was she bussed back to the place an outdated census insisted was her home – an alien zone she fled from – or maybe it was the correct neighbourhood, except her house was destroyed and her family had packed up and left? I see her in my mind's eye, assessing the damage, and setting off on her own – a journey taking her not towards but away from the family with whom she yearned to reunite.

On the Amnesty International website, the Tamil poet Cheran explains he has 'no naive hope or belief that my poetry can turn the world upside down'; nevertheless, 'words and imagination are my weapons. I have no other. There are several poems in my collections on disappearances evoking the friends I have lost.' Even his more atmospheric, less clearly political poems speak of yearning and loss:

> Ask
> me,
> when the last train of the evening has gone
> and the railway lines shiver and break in the cold,
> what it is to wait with a single wing
> and a single flower.

Those women in the shack preferred to know once and for all that their children were dead, rather than go on waiting. In grief-work and trauma parlance, it's called 'closure'. But it was also a basic kind of responsiveness and respect they were after, from the government: a restored commitment to a world of fact in which people are, or are not, dead, where they don't horribly hover in our minds between one state and another, like Schrödinger's cat. A place where their death, if that's the case, is recognised within national history, even if only by a statistic that few outside or indeed within the country will ever read.

A few years ago, I read poems at a poetry festival. The auditorium, from the stage, was pitch-black: I couldn't see anyone. No faces, no bodies, only the heat and shine of the spotlight on my face, shoulders, the page on the lectern crawling with words that no longer seemed mine. A language that – in that moment – seemed as alien to me as Tamil. I spoke into a void, and out of that disproportionate pause between speechlessness and speech (it was my turn to perform, to appear, the audience was waiting for me, it was wrong to delay, hem, haw, vanish into myself) emerged the roar of silence, of time itself passing, pushing me to one side.

Trying for a sentence about this that seems true, I realise I'm thinking of both a passage from George Eliot's *Middlemarch* and a trip I took as a teenager to Greece with my parents. I was so unhappy then: ashamed, those sunlit weeks, of my overweight brown body and acne-riddled face. There was only one moment of relief, when my mother and I sat on the end of a pier past nightfall and became thankfully invisible to ourselves and each other. All we heard was the loud roar of the invisible sea. 'If we had a keen vision and feeling of all ordinary human life,' writes George Eliot at the end of *Middlemarch*,

> it would be like hearing the grass grow and the squirrel's heart beat, and we should die of that roar which lies on the other side of silence.

There are moments when prose turns to poetry; when, reading a novel or a story, a sentence acts like a trapdoor you tumble through into a history previously unglimpsed, or (it could be one and the same) the injured textures of your own life. The eye that skims from page to page is swapped out, you feel it has to be, for the ear that listens. After over three hundred pages of realist prose about life in a mid-nineteenth-century Midlands town, Eliot writes a sentence of prose that's also a line of poetry. As sounds converge ('grass' and 'grow', 'hear' and 'heart beat'), time itself becomes audible; 'silence' itself sings, rhyming with 'like', 'die', 'lies' and 'side'. Reading this passage by a Victorian novelist, I'm once again with my mother at the end of that pier in Greece, past nightfall – listening, listening.

Eliot's thinking about how countless unattended acts of goodness make up the world; of the lives, and aspects of lives, that don't make it into the stories we tell. How little it's possible for us to actually attend to, though we yearn to tune in to a wider range! But we can only live through self-containment. We limit the field of our attention or have it limited for us, either by the apparatus of perception or by the culture we live in, whose news updates are typically about that culture, people like us, people not so far away (from being us).

This is an experiment in talking about those women in that shack and what they felt, through talking about myself and how I once felt. It's an experiment in not being ashamed of my own 'First World problems' (a phrase Teju Cole disparages, for it makes it sound as if those in Nigeria live only from crisis to crisis, that they don't, too, get frustrated at their cell phones for crashing): a risked connection between the diasporic immigrant and those who've suffered more intensely than I'll ever – than you'll ever – know.

Onstage, I began to apologise for my poems. Poets shouldn't do this. It's one thing to be self-deprecating, and another to suggest your audience shouldn't have bothered coming out (paying to do so, probably). As Eliot suggests, we've a limited attention span, so if you've nothing to say, get off the stage; then a community rarely represented can have one of their own in the spotlight. I don't like the pressure on minority poets to be ostentatiously 'empowered', to be always shouting, in my case, 'I'm brown and I'm proud'. But I also feel the pressure to represent, with some kind of eloquence; this can fade, degrade, into an obligation to entertain; you become a sort of minstrel figure. I was abject that day, asking forgiveness for my brownness, for my presence onstage, for the content and style of my poems. Trying for contact, in that darkness, with a face I might see nod, or hear signal assent or appreciation, I felt in the end completely alone.

I had a period in my life of intense distress, which saw me take several months off work, then move to the Midlands from the North East, where – in the run-up to, and the aftermath of, the referendum vote – I experienced in the street the increasing racism of English culture. People didn't look at me in the same way any more, nor, when I spoke, could they process what I was saying except through a scrim of media-fermented resentments (or, the determination to *not* be like this, to smile and nod at whatever the brown man said). Desperately seeking solutions – a style of invulnerability – I tried so hard to be likeable, biddable. I took to going around with an exaggerated smile on my face, just in case strangers on the verge of violence could be pre-empted by this overt communication of my harmlessness. One day a bloke actually parked up, beckoned us over and complimented me on my good cheer. It was then I knew I'd become, as at that reading (dissolving my presence in jokes), the unthreatening minstrel I mentioned.

My wife and I had a terrible argument about house-buying, in the snooty area where we lived and no one spoke to us – where schoolboys snickered as they passed me on the street. 'It's because we're the only renters,' she said; I struggled to forgive her for disbelieving my alternative explanation. It seemed that we lived in two different worlds, that she couldn't understand the changes in my life linked to seismic convulsions in national culture. This crept, too, into my teaching. My students seemed to me then, for I'd lost the confidence to draw them out, fiercely, determinedly passive. I wanted a conversation: they craved a mansplainer, perpetually sure of himself as I could never be, someone who'd keep them safe. When I did talk at length, they broke eye contact, typed everything down; should I ask a question, their faces went dead. I'd lost confidence. Studies reveal that students in their evaluations are consistently harder on women and minorities; they don't mean to be, I'm sure most aren't racist (quite intensely the opposite, in my experience), but such are the workings of unconscious bias.

I felt, all in all, like the hallooing boy in Robert Frost's 'The Most of It', who finally gets his response when his voice (it's absurd really, though beautiful: a scene from a *Road Runner* cartoon) disturbs a landslide that kills him; prior to this, when he calls out in the dark, there's no answer:

> He thought he kept the universe alone;
> For all the voice in answer he could wake
> Was but the mocking echo of his own
> From some tree-hidden cliff across the lake.
> Some morning from the boulder-broken beach
> He would cry out on life, that what it wants
> Is not its own love back in copy speech,
> But counter-love, original response.

He's a shade arrogant ('He thought he kept the universe alone'), in wishing to become entirely self-sufficient. I have this in me, derived from our economistic, hyper-competitive culture, no doubt, and also from how my parents conceived of our immigrant place in it: when I tried to tell them how sad I'd become, they said, 'Just keep achieving, writing things, stay ahead of the pack.'

So was the problem in me, or outside me – or both?

When you try to talk to people about racism you've experienced, they've a myriad ways of closing (you) down. Some methods are well documented, others less so. If minorities, and women, don't always speak up, it may be because they don't want to have a go at it only to be rebuffed. It may feel better to not say anything, so you can continue to fantasise that if you ever did, the world would respond. In this way, we're like abused people, who'd rather believe it's all their fault than consider the possibility of someone (a parent, a partner) being incapable of loving them.

It can be the case that when a person of colour tries to share their experiences, sometimes even those on the Left, white people who announce themselves in the abstract as anti-racists, don't listen and respond. Sometimes, when I tried telling friends what I was going through, they, constrained by that kind of white progressivism so terrified of saying the wrong thing, didn't have the ears to hear. I'll call this phenomenon, riffing on white fragility, 'white freeze': the moment or hideous duration where a person of colour raises issues of race, and well-meaning white people seize up, go silent, their eyes widen and their faces drop and they say nothing, lest they embarrass themselves by this micro-sojourn out of their own lane. This leaves said person of colour feeling unvalidated and rejected. More silence. More darkness.

I'm thinking still of those women petitioning the Sri Lankan army for news of their children, and being ignored; I'm trying to draw connections; you're free of course to find this an implausible stretch. For an equivalent embarrassment (swapped rapidly for outrage) occurs when one compares sufferings of vastly different scale. I do want to provoke you a little here. Let's begin with the absolute nadir of self-pity: those celebrities who, during the coronavirus lockdown, posted videos of themselves crying in mansions they were unable to leave. People were outraged. But why, I wish to ask, are we so angry; why rush to call them out for being oblivious to the far greater pains others suffer, as if shouting at these *idiots* (from the Greek, for non-practitioners of democracy, non-citizens) will make things better? Why, in short, the cultural move towards using the experiences of some to contradict the experiences of others? Is it a justice-instinct, or does this policing of sadness express only our uncertainty, which ferments into rage, concerning how we relate to each other, or don't, or can't, in a massively unequal multiculture?

This sits close to what Reddit, the ubiquitous news aggregator and discussion site, calls 'gatekeeping'. I find a literary example, and a window on South African apartheid and its legacy, in Ingrid de Kok's poem 'Small passing', whose epigraph says it's written for '. . . a woman whose baby died stillborn, and who was told by a man to stop mourning, "because the trials and horrors suffered daily by black women in this country are more significant than the loss of one white child".' Although it's unlikely, dear reader, that you're South African (if you are, hello!), I suspect so much, here, is as familiar to you as it is to me. The gatekeeping of emotion, the imposed hierarchy of legitimate and illegitimate sufferings. Complications abound as a man, who couldn't experience this grief in the same way, tells a woman she's in the wrong, and I do wonder at de Kok, a white poet, for prioritising gender over race, for would it make a difference to us if that man were definitely Black? Nevertheless, the poem strikes a moral stance, standing up for the bereaved woman by borrowing his voice and turning it inside out:

> In this country you may not
> suffer the death of your stillborn,
> remember the last push into shadow and silence,
> the useless wires and cords on your stomach,
> the nurse's face, the walls, the afterbirth in a basin.
> Do not touch your breasts
> still full of purpose.
> Do not circle the house,
> pack, unpack, the small clothes.
> Do not lie awake at night hearing
> the doctor say 'It was just as well'
> and 'You can have another.'
> In this country you may not
> mourn small passings.

In the movement from 'you may not / suffer' to 'you may not / mourn', de Kok addresses both private pain and the public display of it. The public dimension of grief, its validation by a community, is often essential for us to move on.

O f course the travails of a diasporic Sri Lankan Tamil, a second-generation immigrant, in an increasingly racist England don't compare with actual deaths 'back home' (to use my parents' phrase). I sense the accusation, I make it myself: *you can't compare these things. You're not the same as those people.* But I'm curious about the refusal to countenance a connection between disparate experiences – a route by which empathy could travel. We have to use what we have to try to understand others, even those who've attacked us, perhaps out of their own merited feelings of pain and insecurity.

So there I am, stood in the dark or sat before the silence of others, afraid no one's listening, that the world's growing more and more hostile; and there are those women in their shack, launching at a faceless wall of bureaucracy questions about their dead to which no one in power pays the slightest heed.

T he darkness my voice disappeared into that day, reading my poems onstage, could to some extent be medicated away (I was put on antidepressants); it could be partially explained without reference to racism or the intergenerational terrors which, like a set of rogue genes, get passed down from Tamil parents to their children. My counsellor suggested my mother was overattentive to me as an infant. As soon as I declared a need – maybe, even prior to this, before baby Vidyan began to cry – she rushed in to placate me. As a result, I never learned to entrust myself to the darkness which, should I only hold out, would conjure her, a duration in which I might learn to self-soothe. Instead I came to feel that, without an immediate response, I must be alone.

Sleep-training our baby Frank, it was agony to hear him wailing in the dark (and see him crying and writhing in seething, pixellated greyscale, on the baby monitor) – beyond loving my son, I identified with him. His feelings were too close to mine. I sat downstairs, in the light, while he sobbed upstairs, in the dark. Before he was born, we never thought we'd be parents to let our baby 'cry it out': in fact, we agreed with the psychoanalytic politics of writers like Penelope Leach and Philippa Perry, who suggest that children left to sob in pitch-black, when they do eventually fall asleep, have simply learned to give up on their parents, a decision that may affect how empathetic they'll be towards others later in life. But it soon became clear that going in to console Frank only made it worse: he had to be left to face and surmount this hurdle himself. We tried to be happy downstairs, to watch television, though really our eyes kept darting to the baby monitor. It produced a deep guilt, that I'd like here to connect – again, an experiment – with the diasporic situation. In this model, Frank becomes like those women in Sri Lanka, struggling to be heard, and my wife and I, downstairs, in our cosily lamplit sitting room, are like those of us in the West, quite unaware of atrocities in the Global South, and indeed enjoying luxuries predicated on exploitation of those regions. Looking at the monitor and seeing him in pain and fear was like glancing at one's phone, and reading of distant events one wishes in some way to cure, by getting angry about them, even by opinionating online, feeling all the while an immense powerlessness to actually help.

We don't have to subscribe entirely to the tenets of psychoanalysis to recognise that, in desperate times, the terrible fears of our childhood have ways, mysterious ways, of resurfacing. Alfred Tennyson, mourning his friend Arthur Hallam, describes himself as a hapless baby:

> Behold, we know not anything;
>   I can but trust that good shall fall
>   At last—far off—at last, to all
> And every winter change to spring.
>
> So runs my dream: but what am I?
>   An infant crying in the night:

An infant crying for the light:
And with no language but a cry.

My parents overprotected me, as immigrants often do. The overprotected child comes, first, to believe they're fragile, that they require such protection; second, they grow up feeling the world's full of dangers (it is, but the child's in danger of misidentifying these); finally, they may sense they're a risk to themselves and require perpetual oversight. They seek out protector figures, rituals keeping harm at bay; the Strange Situation, an experiment in which a mother leaves the room, and when she returns, her child may not go to her, but instead attend ferociously to a toy, announcing silently that he doesn't need her, suggests that if distraction can be a neurotic symptom, so too can attention: a too-intent focusing on the task at hand, self-loss through workaholism. Sometimes I wonder if even my ability to focus closely on a poem, to rediscover through it another way forward, has its root in a deep unease.

'Everything happens for a reason,' says my mother – her Hindu fatalism chiming uncannily with Tennyson's cobbled-together theology – and as a teenager this enraged me. 'That's such a middle-class, privileged thing to say,' I shouted. 'What if your grandson Rahul were hit by a car and left in a wheelchair for the rest of his life? What would be the reason for that? And what about all those people who died in Sri Lanka?'

Objecting to global injustices, or inequalities closer to home, there's the danger – I see it in myself and my left-progressive peers – of becoming locked in a position of righteous indignation. It's correct to be angry about things, but that doesn't remove the danger of being pushed by our politics back into the grievance-posture of a teenager. There's a brave moment – a moment vulnerable to such indignant accusation – in Solmaz Sharif's *Look* where, discussing the invasion of Iraq and the killing of innocent civilians, she suggests that she too, an Iranian American, has experienced war:

According to most
definitions, I have never
been at war.

According to mine,
most of my life
spent there.

The second stanza hasn't the confidence to really push through the
equivalence. It's a clipped blurt, such as I, losing my sense of myself,
began to specialise in. Sharif also suggests that war is both a state of
mind and a place: 'most of my life / spent *there*'; is she saying that, as
the child of immigrants, she feels for their homeland too?

There is a trend now, to leap to criticise others, and ourselves,
for comparing petty injuries with real atrocities. But I wonder
if the critique of self-pity is itself laced with self-pity; if, damning
appropriation, we're rushing to cover up in ourselves emotions
dwarfing, in their overweening rancour, any one reference point or, as
T.S. Eliot has it (criticising *Hamlet* for this), an 'objective correlative'.
If, moving to Keats, 'imagined grievances' can hurt more than real
ones (a prompt to action in the moment, these have a built-in end
point) then intense feelings deserve our empathy, no matter how
oblivious of otherness they seem to be. And so Sharif suggests that
as an Iranian American subject to both interpersonal racism and
governmental hyperscrutiny, she is at war.

Tennyson (skipping back) was a racist – ranted to Gladstone that
people in the colonies deserved to be shot – and he's also not the
most fashionable poet ('Alfred Lawn Tennyson', James Joyce called
him). Because my father memorised and learned to love his poems
as part of his colonial education at a Jesuit school in Batticaloa, of
course I argued, growing up, that Tennyson was mellifluous sham.
But I was teaching recently a poem by Sujata Bhatt that mentions
him, and my student Sophia Gatzionis made a wonderful point,

about the transferability between cultures of unspecific melancholia: feeling-states, which, in Tennyson, seem overkill, but may clarify for the reader a very different sort of life. In other words, it's precisely because Tennyson's emotions are excessive, his self-pity without terminus, that he's able to communicate across divides. We see this in Bhatt's poem about her grandfather, 'Nanabhai Bhatt in Prison':

> The next day, he lands in prison again:
> thrown in without a trial
> for helping Gandhiji,
> for Civil Disobedience.
>
> One semester in college
> I spent hours picturing him:
> a thin man with large hands,
> my grandfather in the middle
> of the night, in the middle of writing,
> between ideas he pauses to read
> from Tennyson, his favourite—
>
> *A hand that can be clasped no more—*
>   *Behold me, for I cannot sleep,*
>   *And like a guilty thing I creep*
> *At earliest morning to the door.*
>
> What did he make of the northern trees?
> The 'old yew', the chestnut . . .
> and the strange season of falling leaves
> that comes every year—
> Did he spend hours trying
> to picture it all?

What galled me about my father's love of Tennyson was it felt like a native's infatuation with the Glory of English Literature itself – a fossilised idea of white greatness. How else could he leap the distance between his world and Tennyson's?

But it's precisely this adventure of the imagination for which Bhatt's poem clears a space. She thinks her grandfather was capable of it: she takes his love of canonical British literature seriously (mentioning, also, that 'as a student in Bombay / he saved and saved / and lived on one meal a day for six months / just so he could watch / the visiting English Company / perform Shakespeare'). The overflow of Tennyson's grief for his dead friend, feelings connected with those which, in poems that *aren't* elegies, he indulges to excess – all this could be felt over again by an Indian man imprisoned for his politics. It spoke to him: 'In Memoriam A.H.H.', that long, tendentious, uneven, mournfully recircling poem, in the work it does on the page with Arthur Hallam's death, created an atmosphere of feeling that Nanabhai Bhatt, imprisoned thousands of miles away, and alive in another century, and who never knew Hallam, could nevertheless share.

Sujata Bhatt 'spent hours' in college picturing her grandfather; she wonders, did he 'spend hours' trying to picture Tennyson's landscapes – using the same word, the same verb, as Sharif: 'most of my life / spent there'. To spend time is to use up our lives. And Bhatt suggests there's no better expenditure than hours or even years of trying to understand other people:

> And I spent hours
> picturing his years in prison:
> Winter 1943;
> it is dark in his cell.
> He is sixty years old.
> I see him
> sitting cross-legged on the floor
> and I wonder what he knew
> by heart, I wonder
> which lines gave him the most comfort.

Thinking of those Tamil women – they must imagine obsessively the horrors their vanished loved ones went through, possibly in prison, like Nanabhai Bhatt – I hear an emphasis differentiating 'hours', in the first line, from 'years' in the second. This is the moment where the poet recognises the difference in stature between her grievances and her grandfather's: it's the difference between mere hours and sheer years.

I also pause at the line ending on 'knew'. Nanabhai Bhatt, like my father, knew Tennyson by heart (he wouldn't have had a copy of the poems in his cell). But 'I wonder what he knew' reaches deeper than that. Rather than presume she knows better than her Tennyson-loving, Shakespeare-obsessed, Anglophile grandfather, Bhatt wonders if he actually 'knew' something that she, to this day, doesn't: that you don't, and I don't. She also writes bilingual poems, where the italicised material would be Gujarati: in this case, the foreign substance in the poem is a stanza from Tennyson. How much foreignness, strangeness, can a poem – can any of us – admit into ourselves, into our lives and behaviours, without losing what's essentially us? Or is there no essential me (or you), only this space where ideas, languages, power circuits, cross? Best, then, to keep our borders open – for good.

And like a guilty thing I creep.

In *The Seasons of Trouble*, her study of the Sri Lankan civil war, Rohini Mohan contrasts the lives of detainees subjected to torture, sexual abuse and coercion, with those of their parents and other loved ones trying to find out where they've been taken, but also, trying to continue living, from day to day, and even turning, to this end, their petitionary visits to the relevant authorities into a type of religious ritual, a gesture of observance rather than a genuinely investigative claim – they'd long ago learned no response was forthcoming. Hindu fatalism plays its role: that all is in the hands of the gods is an idea chronically accessible (as research psychologists say of our obsessive thoughts) to people suffering the whims of faceless authoritarian power. As well as the thousands of civilians killed by misdirected shells or fired upon by the Tigers for trying to remove themselves from the northern war zone, Sri Lanka also had to come to terms, as Frances Harrison observes, with the fact that even those in the south 'lived with the constant threat of suicide bombers, terrified even to let their children walk to school.' The intermixture of local beliefs with fear for one's life can be traced in a psychology that my parents, despite their continuing efforts to erase it, carried with them across the ocean to England.

My uncle stayed behind in Colombo. He'd been imprisoned too, supposedly for helping the Tamil Tigers. He was a GP in Trincomalee, the small town on the east coast of Sri Lanka where he and my mother were born, and which, following the conflict, recorded an unusually high number of widowed families. A middle-class Tamil (this is important, he'd never have made it otherwise), he tried to leverage what authority he had, accepting a reconciliatory role in the community – though it brought on threats.

As a member of the 'People's Committee', he was instrumental in securing the release of several youths accused of anti-state activities in 1983; the rioting of what is now known as Black July saw armed personnel arrive at his clinic – also his home – and begin firing through the front door. The whole family, including his mother, my grandmother, had to leap the fence and huddle in an empty plot before returning to their looted home in the morning. What was remarkable was the sudden (or so it seemed) switch from civility to murderousness, and back again. Sinhalese and Tamil communities lived side by side, they were friends. Then – what changed? – buses were set on fire with people still in them, tyres were forced around Tamil men, constraining their arms so they couldn't get away, and they too set on fire. Then, when it was over, you went round to your neighbours' for tea, and found it served out of your own cups, gone missing during the looting.

Thirteen soldiers had been killed near Jaffna by the LTTE; a mob, in response, convened at their funeral and distributed (gained from the police and army, who were complicit) documents identifying Tamil businesses and homes. Chandragupta Amarasinghe's photographs of Black July were suppressed until 1997; nor was it possible to track him down and acquire the rights to reproduce them here. Yet it is precisely because of the Sri Lankan government's refusal to look into war crimes and other atrocities committed against Tamils that this history must be recovered. So I urge you to find these photographs online (where they are freely available), and I'll describe two at length here.

In the first, we see a rioter, arms upraised, in front of a street fire of Tamil goods and vehicles. The flames look in the black-and-white image so absolutely white it's as if reality is being erased. A smear, a smudge, an injury to the negative: it looks less like flame than a resistance within the very event, to representation. (Again, I think of the obstacles to reproducing the photograph in these very pages). The man's posture reminds me of the 'war victory' sculpture we saw on our travels upcountry, a soldier depicted on a plinth with four sculpted lions (the roaring animal on the Sri Lankan flag; 'Sinhalese' means 'lion-people'), one at each corner.

We don't have to, however, concentrate on the man in his white undershirt and striped sarong who, recognising the presence of the cameraman, makes himself the centre of the spectacle. In front of him and slightly to one side stands another, less carefully posed (one arm has disappeared), looking uncertain, as do the figures to the left with their arms crossed and expressions of restive enjoyment, but also chagrin, on their faces. It could be they weren't ashamed before Amarasinghe showed up. But I'd like to think that even within the mob were hesitations, moments of ambivalence, men and women picking up weapons, putting them down, wondering what on earth they were doing.

Anne Ranasinghe, born Anneliese Katz, lived through as a Jewish child in Germany the Kristallnacht or 'night of broken glass' – a pogrom against her people – and witnessed the burning by arson of the synagogue at Essen. Marrying a Sri Lankan, she moved to that country and was present for Black July. Godwin's Law is an internet joke about flame wars (as they're called), and how, the more heated an argument gets online, the more likely it is that one party will compare the other to Hitler. Nazism, and the Holocaust, represent absolute evils, and to invoke them elsewhere is typically seen as excessive: as when Sylvia Plath, in 'Daddy', compares that patriarch to a Nazi and herself to a Jew. But Ranasinghe's unique cross-cultural experience inspires, in 'July 1983', a poem that dares to find in one atrocity the means for understanding another:

> I used to wonder
> about the Nazi killers,
> and those who stood and watched the killing:
>
> does the memory
> of so many pleading eyes
> stab like lightning through their days and years

Both the killers and the German bystanders are guilty: Ranasinghe moves from the past into the present tense, wondering if the Nazis had to live over mentally, afterwards, a version of the trauma they inflicted on others. Or, more precisely, she says that she 'used to wonder' about this, like Sujata Bhatt spending hours picturing her grandfather's situation. But the past tense means she, Ranasinghe, stopped doing this. Perhaps as war criminals aged, were tried, and died; or once she decided there was no hope for, in them, an awareness of what they did; or perhaps the change of tense registers her relocation from one country to another, as an opportunity for terminating her agonised speculations.

Unfortunately, having moved to Sri Lanka, she finds the event, or a version of it, has rearrived: like a traumatic memory. With emphatic anger – making connections, finding rhymes – she writes out of a *now* that, were it not for her poem, and Amarasinghe's photographs, might have faded into a footnote, a bloodless, unreliable, statistic:

Forty years later
once more there is burning
the night sky bloodied, violent and abused

and I—though related
only by marriage—
feel myself both victim and accused,

(black-gutted timber
splinters, shards and ashes
blowing in the wind: nothing remains)—

flinch at the thinnest curl of smoke
shrink from the merest thought of fire
while some warm their hands at the flames.

The interjection about being 'related / only by marriage' compares
with Sharif wondering if she too has experienced war; and with my
worry, about how exactly we can 'relate' to world traumas without
seeming to appropriate them ('related' refers to actual familial relation,
even as it wonders if the two crises are really 'related', though one is
taking place – the words almost, again, rhyme – 'forty years *later*').The
transposition of Jewish and Tamil trauma, the past and the present, is
felt in Ranasinghe's floating adjectives, 'bloodied, violent and abused'.
Describing the flame-tinged, smoke-filled sky of Colombo, she sees
the firmament as, first, bleeding like a Tamil, then, violent like the mob,
then abused, again like those Tamils (or Jewish people). I linger to stress
how the sky represents Ranasinghe's own impure position; a mixture
she bravely confronts, rather than announcing herself as wholly one
of the good and true and victimised. A particular kind of historical
consciousness is trying in this poem to come into being: subject
positions merge and easy distinctions are upended.

The poet feels both 'victim and accused'.The rhyme's powerful
because, while she has married into this situation, her husband

isn't Tamil and she worries she's on the wrong side, though her gut reactions, shaped by a terrified Jewish childhood in Germany, are those of the 'victim', the survivor who sees violence and instinctively flinches and shrinks from it, rather than seeking immunity through identification with the aggressor. The mixed time signatures in the parentheses (the fire ongoing; also, a view of what's left afterwards, that is, 'nothing') suggest a perspective untethered from local horrors into an all-encompassing territory of fear, occupied both by those who suffer and those who take strength from the sufferings of others.

The bonfire of Tamil goods isn't Amarasinghe's most famous picture of Black July. That'd be his portrait (the right word, I think: it's revelatory, painterly, a window on the soul) of a Tamil man stripped naked and about to be beaten, possibly to death. It's one of those photographs where, as with Kevin Carter's notorious image of a starving Sudanese child eyed by a vulture, one can't but mildly despise the photographer for not leaping in to intervene. Between the blurred gaiety of the men on the right and the abject nudity of the man on the left it feels the witness must jump in, barring the way. The concrete step the Tamil man sits on seems to absorb his thighs like memory foam, making him even skinnier-seeming than he is – starved-looking, he takes on the entrenched victimhood of that Sudanese child, or the photographs we've seen of Jewish people in concentration camps. But it's important to remember that, minutes earlier, he would have been clothed: we don't discover in this photograph anything essential about his personality – instead, he becomes exemplary, a picture of, as Shakespeare puts it in the voice of Lear, 'unaccommodated man', who is 'no more but such a poor, bare, forked animal as thou art'.

I put it to you that there are moments of your life when you *did* feel something of what this man in the picture does (if you like, we can separate the man in the picture, iconic, from the actual man, whose life isn't recorded here). When you felt abject, wholly alone, terrified; when your terror began to morph, beyond the moment of its climax, into the learned helplessness of an animal that, with no other options, stops running and fighting and goes simply still. Because of this, you and I, though we haven't (speaking for myself) survived such an atrocity, have a way into this photograph deeper than connoisseurship and more prolonged than a sad, knowing shake of the head, at man's inhumanity to man, or whatever sententious soundbite one might use to wrap things up and move on from horrors so extreme as not only to jar with one's everyday life but to actively contradict it, rendering our happiest moments unrealities, evasions of what has now been revealed as the baseline of human experience.

Yes, even though you haven't been stripped naked by a mob, beaten by them, had everything taken by them, and even though you're likely not a Tamil, look at the picture. Think your way into it. Try.

Two years after Black July – as I turned one, in Leeds, in the north of England – and five days before Deepavali, the festival of lights, my uncle was arrested along with several other Tamils, and, detained at the naval headquarters, accused of making regular payments to the Liberation Tigers of Tamil Eelam. His life could have been over. But he wasn't like that naked man on the kerb. He was protected – by connections, and by his class. A member of the Sinhalese security forces whom he'd previously treated at his medical practice spoke up on my uncle's behalf. During his detention, this man kept my uncle in his private quarters, and one night, when he had to leave because of rioting elsewhere, he even handed him a pistol and asked my uncle to mind his two small children. It was through another connection – the power of his politically influential father-in-law – that my uncle was eventually released; returning home, he was advised to leave the country, for there was now a strong chance that, in a reprise of Black July, he and his family would be targeted. They lived for three years in exile in Tamil Nadu. My parents visited them, taking me: ill throughout with food poisoning, I remember nothing of the stay.

I do remember our later visits to my uncle's small flat in Colombo, where he lived with his wife, two sons and my grandmother – several people to one room. My aunt worked in IT: their only spare room was crammed with machines for her students. My strongest memories are of the nights when, during the daily power outage, we lit candles and played carom by their flickering light: you aim a counter at coloured wooden discs, trying to get them into the board's pockets, as with a snooker or billiard table. Before playing, my uncle massaged talcum powder into the wood to make it slippery. I remember the smell of it, a sweet smell, and the reflection of the candles in his glasses. I idolised his good-naturedness. Unlike my father, my uncle isn't brooding, saturnine, or (I thought) given to anger. He's a round, jolly man, despite what he went through, what his family went through.

I realised how essential to me this belief, passing into myth, had become, when my mother told me, just a few years ago, that my uncle once beat my cousin Balu with a belt when he misbehaved. How could this be? I couldn't imagine my uncle's jocose face distorted in rage, the belt snapping through the air. Thinking of him, I remembered carom, his autodidacticism (he wrote me about the theory that Shakespeare wasn't really the author of his plays), his love of photography and its high-tech equipment; the beautiful snapshots he took in Canada and Australia (where his sons now live) of both land and sea birds. I cherished the myth – incarnated in him – of a transcendently bumbling, oblivious, soft-hearted goodness which, if it got him through the horrors of the Sri Lankan civil war, would surely protect me from discrimination in the UK.

But the situations we live through change us as people – at least temporarily, if not for good. I look at my son Frank and the thought of striking him makes me sick (but then, so did the idea before he was born, of leaving our baby to cry in the dark). One of my strongest childhood memories is of dashing down our hallway in Leeds, colliding with my father's knee and falling over – of his excessive concern, the tears in his eyes as he took me in his arms, asking repeatedly, 'Did I hurt you?' Only years later did I learn that his father, my grandfather – whom I never met, who died before I was born, who is nevertheless the only person alive or dead I truly hate – used to beat him. Not for any reason: he'd just come home and for a laugh punch his son in the stomach.

At university, I had a girlfriend who'd been abused: shaped by those experiences, imprisoned in them, she struck out verbally and also physically, hitting me on two occasions, once with an open hand and once with closed fists, in the chest. When I told my father, those tears reappeared in his eyes. 'Someone who hits you doesn't really respect you,' he said. The look on his face was irrefutable – it was earned; behind it lay a history I was only just beginning to understand, a history that (let me risk another connection) being attacked by the person in the world who was supposed to love me best perhaps even helped me, eventually, to fathom.

As a child my father once ran away from home. This is what Balu did too. The incident with my uncle and the belt occurred during that stretch in Tamil Nadu – after they were forced to flee Trincomalee by the events I've described. Suddenly they were poor: my grandmother, pensionless, depended on the family; my aunt became a seamstress to make ends meet. In a new country, a new situation, my cousin couldn't take it any more: he disappeared – when he was brought back to the house, in that moment of uncertainty and fear, my beautiful, gentle uncle lost it. He took out his belt, shifting from victim to aggressor.

We speak of appropriation in the arts, but there are more private, secret appropriations. I took my uncle's tenderness, removed it from history, and, forcing a smile, tried to resemble the person I took him to be – so no one would hurt me. That's why the news about him disciplining my cousin meant so much: it contradicted the cardboard cut-out I'd made of him, the grossly simplified angel I'd reduced him to for my own purposes. But that buoyant good humour of his was never an evasion of those furies visited and inscribed on Tamils. His love for his son, my cousin, has outlasted the mistake with the belt. I made a worse error, rewriting my uncle's life – because I wanted to rewrite mine. ■

THE SCARECROW

Diaa Jubaili

TRANSLATED FROM THE ARABIC BY CHIP ROSSETTI

Just at the time of the ceasefire between Iraq and Iran in 1988, an infantry platoon discovered that they were in a minefield. They found that out from Private First Class Hakim, who had stepped on a mine.

They were terrified, but they didn't leave him on his own, at least for the first half of that day. Later, one by one, they started to withdraw, ostensibly to go get help, but each time one of them left, he never came back.

Private First Class Hakim stayed there all alone. He didn't budge an inch, for fear of setting off the mine and – at a minimum – losing his leg. That is, if the mine didn't turn him into a pile of body parts.

As time passed, once word had gotten out that the war was officially over, the area where he found himself planted was marked off with barbed wire and warning signs indicating it was a minefield. Farmers returned to their fields and restored them, planting different kinds of crops until they turned green and ripened. After all that, among the scarecrows in the neighboring fields, Private First Class Hakim became known as the Minefield Scarecrow.

Those other scarecrows saw him shooing away crows and eagles, to keep them from carrying off the bones of the platoon members that had lain scattered in the field for years, those who left but who never came back. ■

© TOM HAMMICK
The Unending Sky, 2020
Courtesy of Lyndsey Ingram Gallery

ABBANDONATI

Rory Gleeson

On 4 January 2020, a few days after the New Year celebrations, I returned from a trip around Sicily to my girlfriend's parents' home in Pizzighettone, sixty kilometres or so south-east of Milan. After picking us up from the train, her parents suggested we might surprise her uncle with a visit to the provincial hospital where he worked nearby. Her father dropped us at the small entrance. We walked past a distracted receptionist alone at her desk and strolled down a long corridor. The hospital was sleepy on that winter afternoon, almost completely empty.

Coming from Ireland and the UK, where even the mention of a hospital is a cause of stress, it had a welcoming feel to it. Quiet, and relaxed. There were the usual laminated sheets of medical advice tacked up on the walls. Directives for handwashing and the proper procedures for discarding used needles. Pictographs and signs for counselling groups. We came to a closed door, through which Fedy's mother shouted in Italian that we'd arrived. A yell came back and we waited a few steps away. A few moments later, a slim man in blue scrubs, sixty years old, came from his office, and immediately descended upon both Fedy and her mother, covering them with kisses and hugs. He greeted me warmly, and as we walked towards a more open spot down the hall, he placed Fedy into what could only be described as a headlock, dragging her playfully along with him as he kissed her forehead. His name was Dr Daniele Dainesi and he was working in Codogno Hospital, which in six weeks would become the epicentre of the coronavirus outbreak in Europe, one of the worst-hit regions in the world. As we stood together he grabbed his niece about the shoulders and gave her one last big hug, the pair of them laughing in the empty hall.

The next time I met Daniele it was June, four months after the outbreak, three weeks or so after the Lombardy region had reopened. I was expecting a frazzled shell of the man I'd met. I'd been told that he'd lost a lot of weight, his health severely impacted after his Covid-19 diagnosis. That he'd spent forty days in isolation, mourning his colleagues and patients, possibly blaming himself for the spread of the virus. But the man who entered my girlfriend's house looked tanned and strong in a navy T-shirt and shorts. Fedy and her mother met him at the door, loudly exchanging greetings. I welcomed him in the office, the coolest place in the house on a hot summer's day. He greeted me happily with an elbow bump and gave Fedy a gift of a handful of masks. We sat and I tried to continue the conversation in my slow and poorly pronounced Italian. He insisted we should use English, if I could just speak a little slowly, and Fedy sat to one side to translate if needed. As we talked, we drifted back and forth between languages, Fedy forced to act as translator as our words failed us.

After our trip to Sicily in January, we'd returned to London and gone back to work. On 21 February, Fedy got word that Daniele had come into contact with the coronavirus at his hospital in Codogno and was now being tested for it himself. It would take a few hours. We lay in the dark in our bedroom, Fedy scrolling her phone and looking up news results for Codogno Hospital, texting her mother. We'd barely been paying attention to coronavirus stuff. That was for other people, elsewhere. There were a few isolated cases showing up in Europe, mostly linked to travel abroad, and the vague threat of it landing in the UK. No one, apart from scientists and epidemiologists, was taking it very seriously. But what was unfolding at Codogno was hugely serious. This small hospital, unknown to the world, was soon going to be a buzzword for sickness and tragedy. By 24 February, the government had quarantined the hospital, then the villages surrounding the hospital. Pizzighettone, two towns over from Codogno, had been left off the list of ten towns under quarantine. The red zone, *la zona rossa*, finished at Maleo, a couple of miles away. Soon though, the entire Lombardy region and then all of Italy would be locked down. People were saying it didn't matter all that much where you were, you'd be locked down just the same. But in the villages surrounding Codogno, it did matter. It was impossible to sleep at night with the sound of ambulances blaring by near-constantly, their sirens waking you as they careened down the streets outside your home and back again, bringing the residents of your town, your friends and neighbours, to a place few thought they'd return from.

I was wary about having Fedy with us as we talked: Daniele hadn't told her anything about what had happened at the hospital. I was worried that he might hold back his thoughts, wanting to spare his niece the details, or be too embarrassed or self-conscious to answer me honestly. I asked him how his health was, how much he'd recovered, if indeed he had at all, from corona. He told me yes, physically, he was better. But psychologically, no.

Many of his friends were dead, he said.

He said it simply. Without minimising it or dramatising it, or doing anything with it. It didn't seem like he wanted to get it out of the way early, or to warn me about the nature of the conversation we were going to have. He just said it. And he talked for the rest of the interview in this way. Simple, factual and heartbreaking.

Their first coronavirus patient, that they knew of, was Patient One. He'd presented with flulike symptoms and been sent home twice due to their relatively minor nature, initially by his GP, then again by the hospital on 18 February. He was seen that day by several different doctors, including Daniele, who couldn't figure out what was wrong with him. No one had even thought of Covid-19 being a possibility. That was way off, half the world away in Wuhan, not in this small hospital outside an agro-industrial commuter town. When Patient One returned to the hospital on 19 February his condition had deteriorated. One doctor, Laura Ricevuti, heard the patient's wife say he'd had dinner with a colleague who'd just come back from China. As he was transferred to a new ward, Ricevuti recommended he be tested for coronavirus. The doctor who returned the diagnosis, Annalisa Malara, would later be interviewed repeatedly on TV and radio. They would both eventually be honoured as Knights of the Republic, heroes. At the time though, Patient One's health continued to worsen, and suddenly the number of patients admitted to the hospital with pulmonary and other coronavirus symptoms was going up, and up, and up. Patient One's original GP fell sick, as did his friends and family. The doctors in Codogno were all tested, but while they were waiting for the results they went to work, treating as many patients as they could.

It was chaos. They set up a clean zone and a dirty zone, but, with so many patients needing help, the staff were moving back and forth between them. In the beginning Daniele was working without proper protective clothing or equipment. There were pictures in the news of Chinese doctors in bodysuits, treating patients like they'd been sent in to defuse a bomb. Daniele was working in a simple face mask, in situations where viral load can have a huge impact on the health and potential contagiousness of a physician. It was almost inevitable he'd get corona, if he didn't already have it. They carried on anyway. And the World Health Organization, the EU, the government . . .

Yeah, when did they arrive? I asked.

They didn't, he said.

Abbandonati.

*

The WHO were helping others maybe. The government was containing things. No one came to help them. As far as he could see, no one cared. He said it again.

Abbandonati. Abbandonati.

In my head I'd imagined big jeeps screeching to a halt outside Codogno Hospital. Men in blue hazmat suits jumping out and ploughing in to sort out the chaos, running past the confused workers to set up triage areas, seal everything off, erect plastic sheets and say, 'We're taking over. Sit this one out.'

No.

Abbandonati.

They had no idea what was going on. By the time help came, it was much too late.

In the first week of March, I went to my boxing club for the last time, having become sufficiently worried about the amounts of biohazard that come with being in a low-ceilinged room with forty other individuals gasping for air, doing push-ups and trading body shots, pools of sweat seeping into the mats under your feet. At my last session, our instructor, answering a question down the far end of the room, yelled, 'CORONA? Mate if you're putting your face on those mats, corona is the least of your worries.' We laughed, because it was funny and he'd delivered it with excellent timing. The club kept running its sessions, though I stopped going.

Underneath a Facebook photo promoting the club's 'senior session' a week and a half later, days before England officially locked down, a few people tentatively asked about the wisdom of continuing such close-contact work during an epidemic. The club's manager replied that they were following best practices, and that other council-run fitness clubs were remaining open. The government hadn't told gyms to close. At that stage the virus had already taken hold in the UK, was tearing silently through its nursing homes and hospitals, with cases and deaths just a few days away from spiking. I disagreed with the manager, could see it was a terrible choice. But also I could see his reasoning. In a time of misinformation and conflicting health advice being shared across Facebook, Twitter and WhatsApp, he trusted the government. Simple.

Sitting in the sweltering office in June, it was clear Daniele was still confused about things, what happened when. He'd known within three or four days that what was happening was going to get worse, that it would spread all over Italy, and the world. His first test for Covid-19 had come back negative so he'd continued working. He can't remember the worst day. It was all bad, and too fast. Patients kept coming, more and more, worse and worse.

What was your main priority, I asked him. In the first days of the outbreak, were you trying to treat people, or get them out of the hospital so it could close?

Priority? There was no priority. There was no time to think, no time to prioritise anything. They were just trying to treat as many as they could. They were on double, triple shifts. No time to sleep or rest. And it was getting worse. Somewhere in the middle of it all, they must have started to receive help, though Daniele doesn't say when.

There was a line of ambulances, he said. Waiting to get into the hospital, so they could drop off patients and return with more. The line stretched down the road. He'd never seen anything like it.

Cuban doctors would eventually fly in to help them, to replace the Italian physicians who were coming down with Covid-19. Médecins Sans Frontières arrived, Russian military doctors. There were issues with translation, so they worked in English. I wondered how they'd managed to coordinate life-or-death medical care while trying to mentally translate from Italian to English, English to Russian, then back again.

As people came in with symptoms, their chests were X-rayed. One day, 200 people's X-rays showed they needed intensive care in order to survive. They didn't have enough space or equipment, so the doctors decided who to treat based on age. The youngest were given care. The old were made comfortable and left to die on beds in the hallway. Their bodies would be taken from the corridors and put straight into coffins.

At one point Daniele went to the mortuary and found it filled with coffins. Enough that he couldn't open the door all the way to get in. Too many to walk around the floor. Soon after, he tested positive for Covid-19. He already had a fever, and was working knowing he probably had it. It didn't matter. All those he was treating were infected.

He left the hospital and went home to isolate alone in his apartment in Lodi. He didn't tell his mother he was sick. He told Fedy's mother, who was texting and ringing him daily, that he'd been misdiagnosed. He wouldn't answer Fedy's texts, as we sat out and watched the news in London, where life was continuing completely as normal, people making jokes about toilet roll running out, Boris Johnson announcing he was happily shaking hands with corona patients. For the first two weeks Daniele suffered a fever, his temperature wavering between thirty-nine and forty degrees. He'd get calls from the hospital checking on him. A woman two doors down, on whose husband he'd done a knee operation, left meals outside his door every day: lasagne, pasta, meat.

He isolated for forty days. For two weeks he didn't turn on the news, or listen to the radio, or read a paper. The hospital, however, kept him informed about his friends. Doctors and nurses and other workers who were falling sick, their immune systems unable to cope with such heavy exposure to the virus. He stayed in. Alone, on a cocktail of antibiotics, antiretrovirals and antimalarial drugs, his fever out of control, he was afraid he was going to die. Fedy translates this, looking at her uncle. He nods his head. She hadn't even known he was sick at the time. He'd told them it was only the flu.

He sat up one night, on maybe the tenth night of his isolation, thinking about his fellow doctors. He had a fever of thirty-nine degrees. Beside the television were two bottles of Valpolicella he'd been given as a gift. He drank both bottles of wine, his fever running so high he couldn't even taste them. He would never recommend alcohol as a treatment, he said. But it worked for him. It stopped the pain. He didn't feel as much.

One of the things that came from the pandemic were the odd stories that resulted from thousands of people forced into strange, unexpected interactions with the world around them. As we drove to Pizzighettone, Fedy had stopped off in a roadside cafe for a bottle of water and came back reporting that sitting inside was an old man in a World War II era gas mask enjoying an afternoon spritz. In Pizzi we were told stories of patients who'd fallen unconscious in Italy and woken up in Germany, having been transported there overnight due to bed shortages. They came to, in a fever, and thought that the afterlife was being run by Germans. During a lockdown, another said, the latest fashion item in Milan had become a large yellow bag from Esselunga, a national supermarket chain, that could be used as an excuse for an illicit walk. There were accounts of dogs collapsing from exhaustion, having been borrowed for walks by dozens of people. The longer time went on, the more these stories seemed to make up the main narrative of the affected areas. Like the famous videos of people singing from balconies, they were distractions from the obvious pain and tragedy that was taking place. You'd be forgiven for hearing those stories and thinking what wonderful spirit in trying times. I heard them and thought as much. But late into every evening, my girlfriend was on the phone to her mother, who talked for hours about the stories she was hearing from her neighbourhood. Bodies being buried in mass ceremonies. Physicians flipping coins to decide who would receive treatment. Her best friend, a GP in Pizzighettone, begging emergency services every night to send ambulances for her dying patients, but being told there were none available, all were in use.

When we reached the house in Pizzi, as I was inside prepping for the interview, a neighbour in her seventies came out to say hello to Fedy and her mother through the fence. The neighbour's husband was known for his love of the outdoors. After three months of lockdown, of ambulances and death notices, he'd stopped talking. When people called by, he hid from them. Fedy told me that as they chatted to their neighbour through the fence, they saw her husband inside the house and called to him. He quickly left through the front door, climbed into his car and drove off without a word, his wife watching him go. These stories don't warm your heart. They don't help you sleep better at night, or make you want to share them online. They make you want to sit in a dark room by yourself, the lights off, no sound of TV or radio or music to take you away.

While we were travelling in Sicily back in December, six weeks before the outbreak, we'd gone walking around Catania, a beautiful, hot city on the east coast. I was struggling through a flu I'd managed to contract over the Christmas holidays in Dublin. Two days before I'd left for Sicily, the cold my body had been fighting off for the best part of a week finally presented itself. I coughed constantly as I lay in bed or scruffed through the house in a bed sheet feeling sorry for myself. I flew to Italy in a daze, meeting my girlfriend and her parents at Bergamo airport before we boarded another flight to Catania, where I collapsed into bed.

The next morning, though the temperature was into double digits, I was shivering and cold. As we walked through the early-morning streets we passed by a protest. A large group of men were chanting on a street corner. A man with a bullhorn was shouting through the streets, as the men around him held up signs and bellowed. Written on a banner behind them, in large red and black letters was the phrase:

ABBANDONATI DALLE ISTITUZIONI

Abandoned by the institutions.

They'd been fired from a local grocery chain. Let go over the holidays and denied even their back wages. They held signs accusing the local unions, by name, of not caring, of doing nothing. Where were they now when they needed them?

Sitting in front of Daniele, he also used this word, *abbandonati*. The healthcare workers in that hospital had not protested like those men, nor would they. Daniele had repeated that the idea of a healthcare worker as a hero is misplaced. He waxed lyrical about the heroic nature of raising a family instead. I told him of our experience in the UK, where every Thursday night, spurred on by the government, the nation went outside to clap for the NHS, giving them applause, when what they really needed was protective gear. Masks, gloves. Guidance. Structures. Help. The government would clap for the NHS, but it wouldn't protect it.

Daniele shook his head. Their government and Giuseppe Conte, its leader, had early on blamed the hospital at Codogno for mismanagement. For not doing enough to spot the virus earlier, which had led to an increased death rate. They apologised officially the next day, as more and more evidence pointed to the fact that the virus had been dormant in the entire region for weeks, if not months. That Patient One was only the first known case of a huge undercurrent of cases. In Italy and abroad, there was a kind of lurid fascination with Patient One. His details were circulated constantly in news reports and papers, updated endlessly. He was thirty-eight years old. Healthy. Ran marathons. Socialised. He had infected several doctors and patients. There were line graphs and flow charts, a single dot labelled Patient One, which spread outwards and outwards showing those he had infected. Even the phrase used to describe him, 'superspreader', reeked of judgement.

I thought of my own health on that trip around Sicily. I'd taken two flights from Dublin while sick. My nose running while I coughed and my eyes bulged, bloodshot and streaming. During my trip, I'd slept in different people's homes. Played foosball in the middle of a packed hostel. I'd taken intercity trains and local buses. I'd boarded an overnight ferry to Naples, where I drank a beer among a crowd of seventy or so firefighters – critical workers – returning from an official presentation. I'd celebrated New Year's in Palermo, dancing in a crowd of thousands of people cheering and hugging and kissing.

I'd exposed my own family and the family of my girlfriend to what I'd considered a mild flu, and I'd visited Codogno Hospital, which in less than two months would be brought to its knees by a pulmonary virus and subsequently blamed for its spread.

What I'd done, travelling while sick, was not something I'd even considered to be immoral. If anything at the time it seemed like a testament to my strength. Now, retrospectively, it could be considered an act of gross selfishness and stupidity. Patient One had attended three meals and played a game of soccer. Judging him for his unknowing and unwilling role in a crisis beyond his control seems deeply unfair. In any case, the new models showed he was just one dot in a continuum. That there were likely hundreds of dots before him. Patient Zero was never found. They could have been from France, China, Germany, anywhere. Despite this, Patient One's full name and details were leaked to the press and broadcast all over the world. He was an easy excuse, a convenient way to make sense of it all. One guy, a superspreader, had been careless, and now thousands were dead.

In his case, I would say *Abbandonati*. All known details about him were released and reported on again and again. It's so much easier to point to one thing, one person and one hospital, and pin it on them, than it is to address a massively complicated and interconnected series of institutional and political failures. The government had blamed hospital workers for lax standards as they fell sick and died after working near constantly without protective gear, fighting a virus they had very little idea how to treat. Meanwhile in the UK, the government, wary of disrupting the economy, resisted calls to close down, letting packed trains run and pubs remain open. You can still go for a kick-about, they said, just go easy on the slide tackles.

Daniele wasn't angry. At the government, at getting blamed. He was convinced that the WHO had kept secrets, that the government could have done more. But he wasn't angry. He was proud of what he and his colleagues had done for their town and their country, despite the terrible cost. In the first wave, Lombardy accounted for almost half of all coronavirus deaths in Italy, more than 16,000 people. They'd tried to save them.

When he returned to work after his isolation, his co-workers went with him to visit the graves of those who'd died at their hospital. He said he would never go back to that graveyard. It was too much.

I asked him finally about the psychological problems he'd mentioned. About his colleagues. It was then that he told me the numbers, his niece watching. In Codogno, it hadn't been the hospital workers who'd died, but the GPs from the surrounding area, who'd kept seeing patients as the hospital doctors had fallen sick.

At least four doctors from the towns around Codogno had died. In Casalpusterlengo, Maleo, Pizzighettone. Dr Marcello Natali, a GP in Codogno, had died after speaking out about the lack of protective equipment for healthcare workers. He told reporters he'd been treating patients without gloves, using a single-use mask for a week.

More of Daniele's friends and colleagues from different areas across Lombardy were gone. In the first two months of lockdown, more than 150 doctors died, and over thirty nurses. A large majority of those were in Lombardy.

He said he had a *nodo alla gola*, a knot in his throat. It was lodged in at the bottom of his windpipe, and it kept his head separated from his heart, his stomach, his lungs. He carried this knot in his throat with him everywhere. When he thought of his friends and patients. When he'd visited their graves. He said many of his colleagues also had this knot in their throat. Men and women who'd intubated and ventilated those who'd fallen sick. It was there, constantly. They carried on with their jobs same as before, only now with a knot caught deep down in their throats, not letting them breathe.

I wondered if he felt he had changed, if he felt like a different person. No, he said. Not at all. He was just deeply wounded.

There's a field of academia devoted to the study of trauma, reaching across psychology, sociology, biology and world literature. The language Daniele used around the *nodo alla gola*, the deep wound he felt, matched other accounts I'd read about trauma. I asked him if he was aware of the reports of post-traumatic stress disorder in care workers and survivors. Patients who had recovered from the virus, those who'd been intubated, were waking up screaming in the middle of the night, feeling like they were drowning, or being crushed. He said no. No. He just had this knot in his throat. This wound.

I left my attempts at diagnosis there. I didn't see what could be gained by trying to name something so intimate and brutal. He was hurt. That was it. He'd been due to retire next year, he said. But now, he couldn't even think of doing so. The only way he could think of getting better was to keep working, to keep treating people.

Spero, he said. If I keep working, I can heal the wound. If I keep helping people, it'll get better. He didn't look too hopeful, as he added, again, *Spero.*

I hope.

Spero spero, spero spero.

I hope I hope, I hope I hope.

In the months since the outbreak, and in light of the subsequent devastation caused by the virus worldwide, views about the workers at Codogno have changed. Back in June, Daniele had voiced a concern that Italy, in his eyes the centre of culture in the Western world, of history and art and language, had become a laughing stock. That they had been ridiculed and their advice ignored. At the time, I'd seen a lot of memes, from Italians themselves, about the outbreak, and specifically Codogno. In subsequent months, those memes had faded away, as other cities and then countries fared worse than them. The brutal time they had gone through had enabled them to give, to those who had listened, a fair warning of what was to come. Hospitals unable to cope with the sheer volume of patients, health workers stretched too thin as they ran out of equipment, the dead piling up in corridors, in churches and in crematoriums. That lesson came from Italy, from Codogno and Bergamo. The talk became of flattening the curve, which, by and large, appears to have succeeded, if only temporarily.

In the early days of the virus, as Italy locked down but much of the rest of the world did not, Fedy and I watched the news and heard the stories coming out of Italy, and wondered why, around the world, our leaders seemed not to be paying attention. We have elected officials, governments, for a reason – to manage, to look ahead and plan. The region of northern Italy where Codogno is located is relatively wealthy, with excellent hospitals and health care. What had happened to them could easily, easily happen to others. As we came into the middle of March, anyone who knew anyone in Italy was watching the news constantly, and looking around packed streets and pubs in the UK, wondering what the fuck was going on. A Stereophonics concert went ahead, thousands of people pushed in on top of each other. The races at Cheltenham, with tens of thousands of people attending, went ahead. On national television, Boris Johnson bounced around the idea that we could 'take it on the chin' if the virus spread. In practice, that meant accepting countless avoidable deaths, of old people and medical workers. These gestures, of what was said to be a fighting spirit, laughing at hygienic habits gone mad, would be the very thing that accelerated the disease, and they came from the top of the country's leadership. Despite constant warnings from those who were in the middle of a vast emergency heading our way, the message was YOLO: you only live once.

Some countries, like New Zealand and South Korea, reacted early and saved their citizens. Some like Ireland, reacted late but comparatively well, getting things under control. Others, like the US and the UK, did not.

This is what it means to be abandoned. To trust those in positions of power to help you when you need it most, but find that when the time comes, help isn't there, and it's all far too late.

When the first wave ended, experts warned us the worst was yet to come. As winter approached, our governments told us that they were prepared, that we'd be grand. That it'd all be fine.

Abbandonati. ■

Nate Duke

On a Farm near Junction City

Beside the rainy hog shed, the county food bank
forklifts pallets of old bread, blue with deep mold
and tints of February. In our slickers with knives,
we slit packages of rancid buns, pre-made PB & J's,
their special rot an Oregon green – and feed it all
to the pigs. We feed them fetid eggs, decayed
chickens also, but today is bread day. Farm folk
say pig manure is the only kind with a bad smell;
it's the ammonia. We clean the pen with shovels,
push the slimy dreck to the slough. My colleague
and I, we scrape the floor till our filthy tools spark.
This guy's a real employee, speaks good Spanish
to the other hands; so, when he asks, *are you a man
of the herb?* I think I must be; a dim volunteer,
shoveling his way to dinner. All this because
I should've followed some lover to Chattanooga,
or learned to operate the trackhoes in Arkansas,
but instead I'm near the ocean, and broiled thoughts
cool in labor's mute thrum. After a shower, I'll listen
on the couch to the farm's daughter play Chopin,
while a cat I've never met scales my chest, nestles
into sleep. A kind of recompense I think, for lives
we didn't choose, because winter's animal bed
needed fresh straw, or the woodstove in our bunkhouse
grew cold, and somebody had to get up and stoke it.

AL-BIRR ISLAMIC TRUST MORGUE, GREENWICH ISLAMIC CENTRE, APRIL 2020

Gus Palmer

Introduction by Poppy Sebag-Montefiore

I n the first of Gus Palmer's photographs of the morgue at the Greenwich Islamic Centre I can't find the horizontal. The floor tips to the left and if I rotate it right then the stacks of coffins look as though they'll tumble.

Normally, preparing the dead for burial brings volunteer undertaker Kafil Ahmed to the morgue about once a week. During the last week of March and first half of April his commitment became more than full-time. 'It's like a battle,' he told me on the phone this autumn. 'We were constantly fighting the virus. Before we finish one, another phone call comes to collect another person.' His morgue has cool storage for three bodies; he had around four to prepare each day. 'I'm an elderly person. I have a heart problem.' Ahmed's body looks tense, but in the photograph when he has removed his PPE we see the gentleness in his face. 'We do it for Allah,' he told me.

In early April the breakdown of the mortality rate across ethnic, social, economic and geographic divides wasn't yet clear, but Palmer's sense anecdotally was that Ahmed's community in south-east London was being disproportionately affected. He had eight friends, undertakers in other mosques in SE18, who had all contracted the virus. Six recovered, but two of them died.

'In normal times taking photographs of the deceased is against religion,' Ahmed told me, 'but because this was Covid-19 we needed to educate people and give the community some messages to be safe, to take care of their family members, to know that this virus is quite deadly.'

What began for Gus Palmer as a story about the worst of Covid-19 also became a series of portraits of Ahmed. We see his defiance of the pandemic, and the pride he takes in his work. Here's a person risking his life for others. Here's a community taking care of the dead and their loved ones.

'We're purifying the body and making it ready for the person to travel to his or her Lord,' Ahmed said. 'We don't send a dirty body.' In the rituals of prayer and washing is a sense of life in death: a soul journeying to God, and bacteria returning to the earth. 'All mankind, I created you from the dust and I will put you back into the dust,' Ahmed quotes from the Qur'an. 'And I will resurrect you from the dust on the day of judgement.'

Ahmed isn't paid, at least not in this lifetime. For each burial he'll receive the weight of two mountains of Uhud in the city of Medina on the good side of the Judgement Day scales. 'Two mountains are very heavy,' Ahmed says. The burial services take place outside daily life or monetary gain, in a time marked out for reverence, comfort and affection.

Palmer told me: 'Kafil would suddenly take off his gloves so he could get his hands on his phone. He's got all this PPE on and his phone is ringing off the hook.' One of these calls was from Hamid and Allan Yusuf. Their 86-year-old father, Mussa, had died in hospital from Covid-19. They needed Ahmed's assurance that their father's burial would be carried out as he'd wanted.

'From our point of view this is the greatest respect that we can pay to our father,' Hamid Yusuf told me. 'I know that from the time Kafil picked up my father and bathed him, it was all done out of love and respect. The way he did it was as respectful as when he meets people during their lifetime. There's no higher accolade than this.

This person truly is a man of men. For people in grief, like myself, it's so respectful. The way I can explain it is if you walk down the street and see a baby cry – there's stuff inside you as a human that wants to comfort that baby. That's what he does. It's something not everyone can tease out of themselves, but he does.'

Palmer's portraits of Ahmed sit alongside those of other people risking their lives to take care of others. People do this work in ordinary times, only now it's harder, and more dangerous. It's normally invisible; now we see more of it.

We can't look at the last image of Allan Yusuf alone, low in the frame, the grave out of view, and not feel empathy. He's separate now from his father, yet continuous with him. In ordinary times we rarely see photographs of morgues or funerals. Perhaps we're not sure if we want to, or if we can take them in. Looking at these portraits, we get a sense of the love and respect that Ahmed, and the mosque he's part of, gives to the bereaved. ∎

Mosque caretaker Abdullahi Hassan Osman closes the coffin before the drive to the cemetery.
Usually, the family would be present at this stage, but due to Covid-19, no mourners can
come to the morgue, and only five people are allowed to attend the burial.

Kafil Ahmed brings the body of Mussa Yusuf, who has died of Covid-19, to a burial plot in Eternal Gardens, Kemnal Park Cemetery, Chiselhurst.

hmed walks into the morgue in full PPE.

Ahmed at the Greenwich Islamic Centre in Woolwich, waiting to collect a body from the local hospital.

Before Covid-19, Abdullahi Hassan Osman had never set foot in the morgue. After the surge of deaths, he volunteered his help. Osman and Ahmed lift the body of a deceased woman out of the hearse.

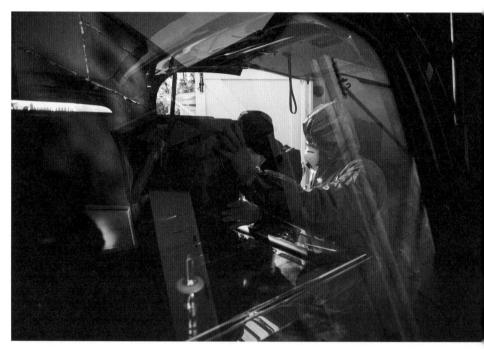

When asked if he was frightened of contracting the virus, Ahmed replied, 'Everybody has to die at some stage. In our religion it is a great honour to bury the dead.'

Ahmed stands in front of the mosque at the Greenwich Islamic Centre. It is the largest mosque in south-east London.

Sitting at his desk in the morgue office, Ahmed collects charitable donations to raise money for families who cannot afford to buy a spot in a cemetery.

Normally, a body would be washed and wrapped in a white linen cloth. Tayammum is the ritual sprinkling of sand or dust on a body when water is not available or other circumstances forbid the normal ritual. In this case, Tayammum obviates physical contact.

Woolwich mosque reflected in the window of the hearse.

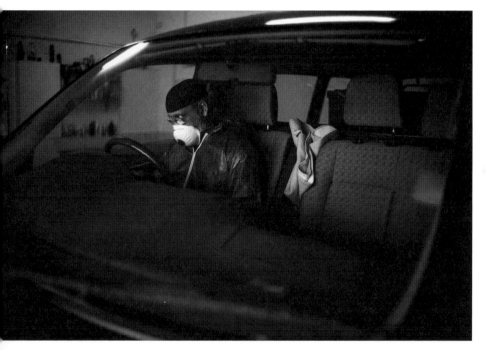

Ahmed at the morgue, having just picked up someone who has died from Covid-19 at Queen Elizabeth Hospital in London.

Hamid and Allan Yusuf (left) pray for their father Mussa Yusuf, who has died from Covid-19.

An imam from another mosque attending Mussa Yusuf's burial at Eternal Gardens.

Cemetery workers help Ahmed lift the coffin out of the hearse. Relatives cannot stand anywhere near the grave for fear of contracting Covid-19.

Ahmed and cemetery workers lift Mussa Yusuf's body into the grave.

Allan Yusuf watches his father being lowered into a grave.

Jason Allen-Paisant

Naming

I

In the wood I hear the beautiful
call of bird I do not know   I wish
I knew the names of birds
and could identify them by their songs

It would be so much nicer to say
I heard the warble of a wood pigeon
as the red floor of the woodland
stretched before me like an avenue
through the high rises of beeches and oaks

as I walk on the path and feel the soft cushion
feel my foot press down into the flesh of the duff

because
a name is
reassurance
a comfort in the flesh
to hold

these songs in the trees
so something could be mine

       warble trill bell fluting?
something nearly right

II

The urge I feel is
to give things names but

   everything is already
named

The urge I feel is
to connect with this land
these plants birds songs
these trees

To name things would be
perverse

perhaps the place within
will always escape the name

In the mind one leaves leaves &
leaves
but on stone earth and grass one stays forever

I have a few trees on my tongue
oak   maple   birch

I have a few birds on my tongue
seagull   mallard   redbreast

I have a few plants on my tongue
rhododendron   English ivy   iris

I have started to see that nothing is itself   everything
turns to something else

like birchbark becoming *vesses-de-loup*
I prefer
    the sound of my wife's ancestors
    the ashes of their throat

like the rhododendron barks becoming
fighting pythons
and me gathering chestnuts for dinner in

a stream that dips below ground
and re-emerges often –
this life –
I no longer know

III

When I go walking in Malham with my wife
there's still that part of me that
   didn't
want to come

that doesn't
want to be in this land
of Karrimor jackets

All I can handle
is nature under fingernails
my grandmother planting
negro yams
shaping the land

All I can handle is the landscape within me
not scenery
spread out on a canvas

Ash Wednesday: 7.00am, 2004/5
Courtesy of Anthony Wilkinson Gallery, London

MY PHANTOMS

Gwendoline Riley

1

When my father died, his sister Mary – his twin – sent me an email. 'Hi Bridge,' she wrote, 'I was very shocked to hear about your dad. I hadn't seen him in a long time but he was my brother and it was a shock. I won't be at the funeral as I don't do "family" these days (not for eight years this Christmas, which I recommend!) but I shall think of you both. I hope you are thriving. Best wishes to you.'

I replied to say that I hadn't seen him in years either, and nor would I be at the funeral, although I didn't know what Michelle had decided.

'Re: the funeral,' Mary wrote, 'I think you're wise. I know it's traditional to share memories at these times so how's this. As Lee was the boy (I was the oldest as you know) he was given the house key when our mum (your nana) started work, and after school he used to run home, to get in the house and lock me out. So I had to do my homework on the step (or walk to our Granny Walsh's if it was raining or cold). Went on for years. Says it all and he didn't change. Best wishes to you.'

*

I was twenty-six then. For eight years I'd been living in London, for six of them in a small flat in Kilburn, with my boyfriend, John. The news about my father was a shock to me, too. I remember the phone call, as John and I were walking up to the station, and how I knew something serious – something bad – must have happened when I saw Michelle's name.

Trying to think about my father now is difficult.

Which thread should I pull?

His being a twin, for instance . . . It strikes me now that that might have had something to do with the way he was. And from such a large family, too. You can see why he might have wanted to set himself apart. But his was a funny kind of distinction, wasn't it? Demanding these pointless tributes left and right. Even when he picked us up, for his Saturday 'access' visits. He refused to ring the doorbell. He wouldn't get out of his car. So one of us always used to have to stand by the window, on lookout. Or anyway, that was what we ended up doing. He'd start sounding his horn otherwise, if Michelle and I weren't out immediately and hurrying down the path.

'There's no point in provoking him, is there?' our mother used to say.

Mary had confided that story about the homework before, more than once, including a detail she left out of the email, but which seems characteristic to me. While she tried to get on with her work, he would lean out of the bathroom window to shout and wave at her. He wouldn't have been taunting her then, I'm sure, or not exclusively anyway, so much as wanting her to celebrate his accomplishment with him. My father saw himself as a sort of beloved outlaw; an admired one-off. He felt himself to be at large in a world which got as much of a kick out of him – out of him-being-him – as he did.

That outlaw's camp was what Michelle and I were bundled into when we got into his car. A rough-and-tumble territory where saying hello was a discardable courtesy, for a start. Instead our father would open with 'Lock!' even as we were pushing the locks down, and then 'Seat belt!' as we were pulling on our seat belts. If the weather looked cold, he might say 'Jumper!', meaning we were to show him that we were wearing one, and if we weren't, by barking the word again – 'Jumper!' – he communicated that we were to go back into the house and get one. 'Haircut!' meant one of us had had a haircut, and would be followed up, as he waited to turn out of our cul-de-sac, with, 'Did they catch whoever did that?' And, 'Hey? Deaf lugs. Did they catch them?'

I remember looking out of that car window. Blank feelings, about home, school, weekends. Here was the golf course. Here were the gasworks. Then the dark minutes under the river. A thudding sound. My father was of a piece with the rest. And his company was something to be weathered, that's all. He had a claim on me – on us – which no one was disputing. Which, in fact, my mother, as was her way, seemed quite excited to uphold. So it was 'Lock!', 'Seat belt!', and then try to let the hours flow by. I'm not sure I even thought of him as a person, really. He was more just this – phenomenon. A gripper of shoulders. A pincher of upper arms. If I was wearing a hat, a snatcher of hats. If I was reading a book, a snatcher of books. Energised bother, in short. And yes, legally mandated.

Unlike my worrying at my mother's psyche, I never had any desire to quiz my father about his life; to interrogate his reasoning. One does come to these peaceful conclusions sometimes. And after all he was no mystery, was he? His nature had to generate satisfaction for itself along the lines I've described. That was it. Getting one over. Being an exceptional case. There was nothing else. With him the difficulty came in dealing with that relentless uniformity of purpose. The way every subject, event or circumstance was used to push towards these same ends. The way his fine musing on his exceptional self did not ever let up. Those Saturdays could feel very cramped as a result.

Apropos London, for instance. Michelle had been on a school trip there with her history class. They'd been to the Tower and the Globe. This information our father attended to as one might a dog's distant barking, before telling us that when *he* first moved down there, he used to spend every weekday evening in an Earls Court pub called the Coopers, which was a 'den of iniquity', but which *he* also called his 'office'. People used to telephone there when they were looking for him, he said, or call in when they needed to see him. The landlady was 'a real old boiler!' he said. But she used to make him chips and egg, which she wouldn't do for anyone else.

I could hardly credit that scene, even aged ten, or eleven: that convivial tableau, with my father blushing at its centre. It sounded like a fantasy of adult life, didn't it? Albeit coming from an adult. Who were all these people, for one thing? And why would they be seeking him out? This was something he'd been impressed by in a television show, wasn't it, or a film? And which he had therefore decided should be his. Or rather, he had decided that it was his. The indulgent community. The local celebrity. I even thought I'd seen that film, up in my room, one Sunday afternoon on BBC 2.

A lot of what he said inspired the same apprehension: that you were listening to someone else's story, not quite cut to fit. He used to call George Harrison 'my mate George!' This because, he said, the two of them had both gone out with the same girl, and had once run into each other at London Airport, when, quote, George was on his way to India, unquote. That one had a second-hand smell. My father also claimed to have been in borstal as a teenager, for the armed robbery of a postmistress. This was certainly a straight lift, bolstering the buccaneering tendency which he found so stirring when he noted it in himself. Later, when I was applying to universities, he told me that at *his* job interviews he always put his feet up on the desk, lit a cigarette, and asked the panel what they could do for *him*. Was that from the television? I wonder. I'm afraid that one might have been taken from life.

It is strange when somebody talks to you like that. When they're lying, but somehow you're on the spot. Was he trying to impress us? But that could hardly be the case: you couldn't value someone's good opinion while thinking they would buy this kind of crap.

And then there was the fact that no one was required to respond to his grandstanding. He didn't notice or care about the absence of questions or comments or of oohs and aahs. I'm not sure he was even interested in our attention qua attention. What Michelle and I – and whichever of his other relatives was about – had to do was be there and be subject to him; we had to not be doing anything else. I'd call that a fit-up job, wouldn't you? And hence that dreadful fixed feeling: that for all that was apparently required of you, you could just as well have been a mannequin. Except, of course, *you couldn't*. A living witness was required for the attitudes of this self-pollinating entity. A living listener was required – and you were it – even as the 'living' element was summarily disregarded.

Nobody ever said anything back. Not once. There were no quibbles, no queries. And so Lee Grant strode untroubled through his subjected realm, where he was, variously, the kindly king and the swashbuckling bandit, the seen-it-all sage and the rude clown, the tender-hearted swain and the blue-eyed boy, and on and on . . . Exceptional cases, every one.

One week, when we got into the car, our father didn't shout 'Lock!' but rather leant back between the seats and, raising his fist slowly, underhand, like celebrating sportsmen do, said, '*Gooooooo* Deggsy!'

Michelle and I were still doing up our seat belts. He seemed to expect us to know who this was, and for us to be as invested in this person's fortunes as he was. We didn't and we weren't, and so we didn't react, although, crucially, we also didn't not react. We did what our instinct told us to do in such moments, which was to sort of fade out of the moment. I found out later that 'Deggsy' was Derek Hatton, a rat-faced local politician, that week acquitted of corruption. For now, in answer to our silence and our bland expressions, our father made his call again, in his darts-referee voice: '*Gooooooo* Deggsy!'

There was still no reaction from us, and our father chuckled when he looked back at the road. What a pair! Not knowing who *Deggsy* was.

That was his opener all day: the pink-knuckled fist raised before him, and '*Gooooooo* Deggsy!' At Mary's house, where we went for our lunch, and then at his mother's house, where we ate our tea. There were no fellow 'Deggsy' enthusiasts forthcoming. Our father was met with the same sort of containment operation Michelle and I had learned to effect: mild smiles while he went on, and then back to what they were doing before. Not that he let that dampen things. Not when he was riding so high. I think he felt 'Deggsy' had scored this point on his behalf, in a way.

As far as his own victories went, my father was generous in sharing his methods. Or at least, it made him happy to talk about them; to pass on what small wisdom &c., &c. I remember one afternoon in Tesco, when we were doing his big shop. He was, as usual, making a point of 'testing the produce', that is, pulling lone grapes from bunches which he wasn't going to buy, and eating them, and then taking a large loose tomato and munching on that as we cruised the aisles. This was a habit of his which made Michelle and me, and me especially, very anxious, which naturally only encouraged him.

'I'm testing the produce!' he'd say, proudly. And then he'd try and cajole the pair of us into walking around munching stolen tomatoes too. This was something neither of us could ever be persuaded to do. Our father had an inhibiting effect in general, a deadening effect, really, for all of his large energy, and these specific needlings and exhortations only ever sent me further inwards. In the supermarket, I remember, I used to try to hang back, behind him, or else I'd get suddenly quite absorbed by a display; anything to drift out of a culpable proximity to his witless vaunting.

On the day I'm thinking of, a summer's day, we were dawdling through the freezer section when he spotted a young woman up ahead of us who was wearing a miniskirt, or a short dress, with bare legs. Our father leant forward over the trolley and sped up slightly until we'd nearly caught up with her, at which point he slowed down, and paused, waiting until she was a little way ahead again, before turning to Michelle and me, conspiratorially:

'What you need to do,' he said, 'is look when they've been to the *toilet*. I noticed this when miniskirts were *first* fashionable. When they've been to the toilet they get an imprint of the seat on their legs. 'You can see it if they've been sitting on a wicker chair as well,' he said, 'or a garden chair, but when they've been to the *toilet* you can see the shape of the toilet seat! *They* don't know it's there. Can you see, there, back of the legs?'

Hotels, too; he got one over on them when he could. He'd once worked on implementing some software, he told us, which enabled hotels to charge customers – 'businessmen' he said – who didn't have the time to check out, by taking their credit-card details in advance.

'Once I knew that,' he said, 'I've never checked out again. If they can do that for businessmen they can do that for me, and if they can't then that's *their* problem not mine!'

He welched on his maintenance payments to our mother for years, in a similar spirit. I know that because he used to boast about it. 'They seek me here! They seek me there!' he'd say.

My father so relished his own triumphs – or the triumphs of people he thought were like him, like Derek Hatton – that it followed (I suppose) that he took an equal, or an equivalent, portion of pleasure in other people's failures. Their disappointments, their humiliations. He could never hear enough about the inadequacy of people who weren't him. And as with his boasting about his past, these things didn't need to have actually happened for him to enjoy them. The fact that he enjoyed them somehow brought them into being, with each innocuous piece of news you shared with him somehow always ending up as a perfect illustration of some risible misstep. Between your mouth and his ear the facts got bent backwards. So he was neither a prospector nor a connoisseur of human shortcomings, really, but rather a sort of processing plant which turned all information into the same brand of thrilling treat: that someone had had a knock-back or that someone had looked a fool.

As we paid our calls, to his sisters, his brother, his mother, Michelle and I were encouraged to share our stories for a second or a third time.

'Tell Chrissie what your mother's been up to!' he'd say,

or,

'Michelle's got this dickhead teacher this year! Tell Owen what you said to him!'

When there wasn't much to tell, no matter. He was ready to take the stand, to give his souped-up version, and then to darken his countenance to make a *serious* point about someone being a 'a *real* creep' or 'a *real* specimen'.

Yes, people were 'specimens', I remember that. And everything they did – their activities, their endeavours, their choices – that was all 'behaviour'. When Michelle started playing football, that was 'behaviour', and her joining Greenpeace was somehow 'behaviour' too. 'No one's impressed by your recent behaviour,' he said, which was another of our father's quirks – to speak not just for himself but rather as the voice, the representative, of some austere adjudicating body.

On it went. Week after week. Through the Mersey Tunnel with his Tom Lehrer tape on loud. And were we listening? Did we get it? He'd rewind it if we didn't!

And who was our mother chasing after now? Hey?

And was our grandmother still obsessed with Margaret Thatcher? Did she still keep rotten food in the fridge?

As we passed the sign for the urban farm in Prenton he'd lower his window and shout 'Mint sauce!' and try and have us do the same.

2

In the Coopers, in 1966, I see my father standing on his own at the bar. On his own with the pools form or the paper, with a pint of Coke on the go. Or I see him on the Tube, smoking away, and regarding his fellow passengers with a keen and bullish expression.

He didn't do badly, to manage a London job and a flat, a girlfriend then a wife, a family of his own – for a few years anyway. He too was accommodated by 'what people did'. By a confluence, too, perhaps, of his particular way of going on and what was happening at the time. He was a forthright northerner, in the era of Albert Finney and John Lennon. Later he was a sort of king-of-the-castle seventies man.

My mother, I think, would have grinned while he talked. All of that spirited scoffing. That spiteful authority. Getting on the right side of that might have looked like a way into something, to her.

Their shared accent would have been an attraction, too, for both sides, I'm sure: setting them apart and drawing them together.

All she would have had to fit herself to then was making sure he always felt so puffed up. That would have been something, wouldn't it, for a person without bearings? I even think it might have made her happy – in the moment, anyway – for here was a game which, if she could never quite win, then she could at least keep playing.

Only she lost her balance there too, somehow. It wasn't quite right. Wasn't quite it. She left him after seven years. She snatched her chance, after some kind of scene with her parents. Proudly, she told me how her father and my father had ended up standing in the kitchen, 'jabbing each other in the chest, yes'.

'You don't talk to my daughter like that!' her father had said. And proudly, shyly, she told me how she had been required to choose by her father, there and then, and how she had chosen him, yes.

'There's no point in provoking him, is there?' she used to say – to repeat – chivvying Michelle and me to find our coats and shoes; to be ready ten minutes before our father was due. Even back then I knew that she was talking to herself, really; whisking herself through the task at hand. My mother had her sayings, but she did not give real advice, ever, about anything.

Here, 'There's no point in provoking him, is there?' seemed to mean, 'There's no reason for me to behave in a sane and civilised way when he doesn't (is there?), not when there's a golden opportunity here for me to join in and be mad too.' And she didn't even mean 'provoking', did she? She meant an omission, not an action. She meant: you mustn't fail to anticipate something he could plausibly decide to be affronted by. Which rather left one with nowhere to go. Michelle and I had never been cheeky or disruptive. We'd been mild and quiet from the start when he was around, and it made no difference. Anything could set him off, or not set him off. All depending on how he wanted to feel; on what kind of satisfaction he wanted to extract. Not provoking him could provoke him. It often did provoke him. She knew that. Why did she like to pretend otherwise? For excitement's sake, perhaps? Or because she didn't want to feel left out? I've an image of a dog trying to join in with a football match, but that's possibly too wretched. I think her mental sleight was more akin to the way Michelle and I, after our swimming lessons, used to hit the buttons on the arcade games in the snack bar: we hadn't put any money in, but nonetheless persuaded ourselves that we were affecting the progress of the yellow lights, which flashed in steps, then slowly cascaded. In fact, there were a lot of children who liked to do that, as I remember. It must be a thing children like to pretend. If someone else had got there first, I used to wait for my turn, not too close to the machines, but not too far away either.

My mother left my father before I was two. I have no memories of my parents married. I would lay odds, though, that, with him, she went in for her fair share of provoking. Proactive provoking, I mean. Because she felt neglected and therefore frightened. Perhaps she told herself he'd find it stimulating, a little bit of pertness, a little show of initiative; that it might lead to a chase or a tickle attack, or some pleasure of that nature, of which she might be the rapturous focus. Would my father have obliged? I suspect not. But I can't say that would have put her off. My mother could be dreadfully hard to put off.

When I think of her now, I think that's what I see, or feel, most of all. Her keyed-up look: fixed on something; fastened on something. A horrible persistence. A sort of mulish innocence.

She was mulish, when she wasn't completely biddable, and each mode always at precisely the wrong time. Like a mime's recalcitrant prop: the door that wouldn't give until it did and sent you sprawling.

3

My aunt Liza was not answering her door. Twice my father had pressed the bell. Now he knocked: a smart tattoo with his knuckles.

Her car was there. She knew she was down to feed us.

'We can guess where she is!' he said, to Michelle, with a chuckle.

A few more seconds passed. Now he bashed on the door, with the side of his fist – as if this were a police raid.

'Huh!' my father said, when there was still no sign of life.

He walked down to the end of the driveway and looked up and down the road. On his way back, he walked behind me, and took my book from my coat pocket. I was reading *Villette*, from the school library. He held it up, over my head, at arm's length.

I didn't reach for it, I stood still, but he pushed me away with his free hand anyway, grinning at Michelle all the while.

'*Ah ah ah ah ah ah ah,*' he said.

Liza was my father's oldest sister. When she appeared, a few moments later, she said, 'Hello gang!' and then stood aside for us to troop in – my father first. He was following his nose to the kitchen now.

'Are we all on lemmo?' Liza said as we took off our coats and hung them up in the hall. From the kitchen doorway I watched her set out four pint glasses and then add ice and a thick slice of lemon to each one. She filled the glasses from a big bottle of R.Whites.

'*Wuthering Heights!*' my father said. And when I didn't respond, he went on, 'That's your mother's obsession. Is it her making you read that?'

By 'obsession' my father usually meant 'interest', if that, but I'd never heard of my mother having any interest in *Wuthering Heights*.

'No,' I said, 'it's from the library.'

'Your mother's one obsession!' he said. 'I never knew what she was talking about! I learnt *something* about it when the BBC did an adaptation. I only watched from pure curiosity. Liza? Did you see that? It was probably up to the usual standards of an adaptation! But the *impression* it conveyed . . . It's really ghastly. Really creepy.'

'It explained a lot,' he said. 'About your mother.'

'Is that her book?' he said.

Liza had made her vegetable curry. When we went through and sat down there was a pot of vanilla yogurt on the table, and some green salad, and half a loaf of sliced brown bread.

'Bridget's brought a book to pose with!' my father said, or called out, as she headed back to the kitchen, but if she heard him, Liza did not follow that up. She came back in with a large pan of curry, and then with four plates, warm from the oven.

'Dig in, gang,' she said. 'Don't wait.'

Liza was the first vegetarian I ever met, and a good advert for the regimen: she was friendly and energetic. She was surely one factor in both Michelle and I deciding that we wanted to stop eating meat. Vegetarianism counted as 'behaviour', of course, so my father had some hay to make with that whenever we were at her house. That if we didn't eat cows there'd *be* no cows; that kind of thing. We *wanted* those animals to go extinct, did we? he said. And there were endless remarks about wind. Still, he always tucked into her food. He would even allow that it was tasty, with one caveat: 'Be nicer with some chunks of chicken!' he used to say. And then, stage-whispering to Michelle and me, he might say, 'Don't worry, we'll get some nuggets on the way back!'

Liza gave no appearance of not enjoying all this. She ate her food, she smiled at Michelle and me.

'So what's the news, gang?' she'd say.

That afternoon, back at his place, I sat where I always sat, next to him on the settee, by the window. Michelle was in the chair with the footrest, having her own thoughts too, I expect.

He watched the same things every week: football, if Everton were playing, otherwise a western on Channel 4, then *What the Papers Say*. Then it was time to go to his mother's for our tea.

No football that day. Instead: galloping, whinnying, gunshots. I'd look up from my book when there was a commotion and see a red kerchief or a cloud of creamy dust.

At a certain point, I became aware that my father was up to something to my right. He was sitting up straighter, and I could see Michelle doggedly ignoring some kind of call on her attention. When I turned to look at him he scrambled to hide something, or anyway to perform trying to hide it, and then to perform looking innocent. It was an Argos catalogue, which he'd quickly pushed under a cushion. Evidently he'd been doing some kind of impression of me.

Later, I put together where he'd got that business about *Wuthering Heights*. My mother liked the Kate Bush song, that was all. She'd sing along if that came on, and do a sort of flapping dance, and if Michelle or I were around, would try and get us to look at her dancing. She must have done the same with him, once upon a time. That's what he'd meant by her 'obsession'.

4

There were two books in my father's flat: an old *Private Eye Annual* and *The Complete Henry Root Letters*. Both volumes sat gathering dust on his bathroom windowsill. But my father was a reader. He was one and he always had been one, he let me know on the drive over the following week.

'I've got thirty-odd years on *you*,' he said, chuckling.

'If we say we both started *seriously* reading at age *eight*,' he said, putting it together for me, 'then you've got five years and I've got thirty-five years!'

'You do realise that I'm a lot older than you, don't you?' he said, chuckling again.

He continued to muse on this long career as we dipped into the tunnel:

'It is *interesting*,' he said, 'at my age, *re*reading is a particular pleasure . . .'

After that, if ever I took a book with me on Saturday, I had to bank on my father snatching it from me at some point. If I were reading on his settee, he might pretend to yawn and stretch, and grab my book. Or on his way back from the kitchen, or the loo, he might walk behind the settee and reach down from above. There was nothing to do but wait then, while he applied himself.

If the writer or the book was one he had heard of he often used to just say, 'Huh!' Almost involuntarily. As if something was repeating on him. Sometimes, too, it was his grim duty to inform me – as one who should really have done her due diligence – that the writer in question had been seen on television by him, by Lee Grant, and deemed a 'creep' or a 'poser'. All I'd had to do was ask. But there it was. On those occasions he would give the book back to me with a pitying frown, it being a meaningless, hollowed-out object now.

If the name was new to him, then he handled the book suspiciously. 'Never heard of them!' he'd say. (His verdict.) And if the book was American, then it was null because it wasn't *Of Mice and Men*. 'Get back to me when you've read *Of Mice and Men*!' he used to say. Or, 'If you were *seriously* interested in that ah, period, then you'd've read *Of Mice and Men*.' Of a Penguin Classic, he'd say, 'Posing!' Or else he would lean in very close and whisper, 'You're *bluffing!*' And here, as with Liza and the chicken chunks, or Mary and the homework, he seemed to expect me to enjoy this too, almost as if it were part of a routine we had going. As if my reading a book in his flat, because it was what I liked to do, and was a way of getting something out of this stolen – or rather, *collected* – time, was in fact some kind of stimulating struggle, laid on for him, by me, to keep his large and restless spirit in good shape. It was the processing-plant effect again.

I did not have any kind of routine going with this person, however. When he spoke I waited for him to stop speaking. When he reminisced about listening to *Of Mice and Men* on the radio when he was a boy, for instance, and how he'd started crying at the end, and how 'Your nana *always* remembered how that affected me!', I waited for him to stop reminiscing.

It was striking how proud he was of his strength of feeling. One would often hear how he'd cried at this or been 'devastated' by that. Here was another distinction, I suppose. I suppose somebody – his mother again? – had remarked on it when he was small, and so up he'd stepped to the role of the sensitive one; the feelingful one.

Sometimes, while I was reading or otherwise keeping to myself, this tender-hearted person would reach over and pinch me, under the ribs, using his thumb and forefinger. He'd keep his eyes on the television. He'd approximate a confused look when I reacted, and if I didn't react, he'd wait a few seconds and then pinch harder. Or if I stood up to go to the loo, and if I was wearing my tracksuit, he might reach out and yank my trousers down.

That impression of me got frequent outings, too. Once with an up-to-the-minute twist: he'd gone out and bought a copy of *The Satanic Verses*, which was in the news at the time.

When we got back to his place, he produced this book, and put his feet up and pretended to concentrate on it, his conception of which activity involved bunching his eyebrows and letting his mouth sag open.

'Have you not brought a book to pose with?' he said, to Michelle, who didn't answer, only shook her head.

'You don't fancy posing like your sister?' he said.

And again, Michelle fixed her eyes on the sky outside, and faded out of the moment, as we'd both learnt to do. She smiled mildly.

'Dickhead,' said my father.

In the world as surveyed by him, there was no shortage of 'dickheads!' And then of course there were his 'businessmen' – I've mentioned them. A type he called 'females' had a predatory intent – these included his 'well-fed specimens', of whom he was apt to remark, when he spotted one, that he wouldn't want to meet *that* on a dark night, and his 'healthy-looking specimens!' – this indicating a striking cleavage. *Sotto voce*, in shops or on the street, he would draw my or Michelle's attention to 'healthy-looking specimens'. Also abroad were 'posers!' (like me) and, more exceptionally, and never seen in the wild, '*intelligent* people'. He used to bring news, sometimes, from the latter constituency. The news was generated by himself, but it was an important recourse nonetheless. '*Intelligent* people' were a respected tribe, like his 'businessmen'.

Their expertise was brought to bear when I was reading my Chekhov, my *Five Plays*. My father had had nothing to say about that book at first; he just tossed it back to me on the settee; tossed it very carelessly, so that it fell on the floor. I even wondered if his interest in my reading hadn't worn itself out. But it wasn't that. It was that he'd decided he'd have to consult on this one. What he'd learnt was revealed on the drive home that night.

'You do know there's no *point* reading things in a translation,' he said.

'Because it's not the original language,' he explained. 'It could be anything.'

'*Intelligent* people learn the language if they're really interested,' he said.

'What you're reading could be anything,' he said, again.

I didn't have much to say to this. I looked out of the window, just as Michelle was looking out of her window.

'Hello?' he said.

Then,

'Is somebody sulking back there?' he said, chuckling.

Next came the tunnel. We slowed for the barrier.

'She's sulking!' trilled my father.

I watched the tunnel walls. Then we were out again, in Wallasey. Here was the golf course, and then our old school.

'How's your ring, Bridget?' my father said. 'Is it itchy?'

'I've been meaning to ask you if your worms had come back,' he said.

I had had worms when I was little. It came from not ever washing my hands. He often brought it up.

'I think you need to put some cream on your ring,' he said. 'It must be very itchy.'

'It must be very itchy,' he said, 'from the look on that face.'

'Do you think *Madame*,' he said, speaking in his la-di-da voice now, 'might find some time when she's not posing with Russian books to put some cream on her itchy ring?'

Such was the flailing of Lee Grant. But he couldn't be discouraged. His system ran on whatever it could get or on nothing. The following week he announced that he'd bought tickets for a Chekhov play: for *Three Sisters* at the Everyman. He'd bought two tickets, just for me and him, not for Michelle.

'Well you're not interested are you?' he said.

'I don't know what it is,' Michelle said.

'Well, you're not interested then are you?' he said, sitting back in his chair, pushing his plate away for Mary to get. 'I'm not going to waste a seat on someone too thick to understand it. It isn't a pantomime.'

'If I was going to a pantomime I might take you,' he said.

'But this is *Chekhov*,' he said.

5

The Everyman bar was noisy, and smoky. The stairs were busy. We carried our pints of Coke carefully to our seats.

My father was looking around, assessing the audience. After a moment, he leant in to whisper, out of the side of his mouth,

'Healthy-looking specimen at one o'clock.'

And then, nodding to a man in front of us who was wearing a greasy silk scarf, 'Now that's a very typical *theatre* look, there,' he said. Again, he lowered his voice to pass on this intelligence. 'A very *thethpian* look,' he said.

A few hours later, as we left, he told me about the play, repeating things we'd both read in the programme.

'The thing you have to remember,' he said, 'is Russia is *huge*.'

'It's a really big place,' he said, seriously, almost angrily.

Back at his mother's house, he turned around in his chair to tell her all about it, too; to tell her the story while she served up dinner through the hatch.

'I had to stop myself at one point!' he said. 'There's this woman, the brother's wife, and she was such a bitch, so *cruel*, I had to stop myself just standing up and shouting!'

I can see him there. Knife and fork at the ready. All innocence. All enthusiasm.

That Russia was 'huge' became one of a handful of facts or commonplaces with which our father liked to barrack Michelle and me. It sat alongside rabbits-from-the-hat like 'tomatoes are a *fruit!*' and that the composer Verdi – Giuseppe Verdi – was 'called', in English, 'Joe Green!' That '*really* intelligent people don't go to university' was one, and, more unexpectedly, that 'of course, maths is really philosophy, if you take it far enough'. This was a pearl he regularly encouraged us both to share with our maths teachers, with the idea being, I think, that we were then to report back to him on the mind-blown admiration it had drawn.

I wish things had ended there, with Chekhov. They didn't. The following week, instead of heading to Nana Grant's at five o'clock, Michelle and I were back at the Everyman, sitting with our father in the Bistro, with heaped plates from the canteen buffet and pints of Coke. Our father hadn't given a reason for this excursion. He'd only said, 'Change of plan!' And then, though we hadn't followed that up, he'd said, 'You'll see!' and, tapping the side of his nose, he'd said, '*Ah ah ah ah ah ah ah.*'

I liked it there, though, down in the basement. I'd never eaten anywhere like that before: a loud, grown-up place, with garlicky smells and cigarette smoke; with confident conversation, friendly laughter, and wine drunk casually from small glass tumblers.

In the toilets there were old theatre posters pasted over each other on the walls and doors.

One of the girls behind the bar had pink hair in a plush bouffant.

The food was all new to me, too. Pasta twirls with chilli bits and wrinkly black olives (instead of Dolmio sauce) and a little fluted tureen of hummus, and some sort of broccoli bake, all dished out on the same plate, like school dinners – in that one respect. The people standing at the bar wore overcoats and boots and their long hair was crimped or teased, like the stars of certain films or pop videos I'd seen. My father kept saying 'Student!' as if it were a game to identify them. As if he were calling out 'Snap!' He said it when you were in the middle of a sentence, after he'd asked you a question.

We were sitting at the end of one of the long communal benches. While we ate, my father kept looking over my shoulder, moving his head, half standing up. He was trying to catch sight of the entrance, I realised. And then suddenly, hands on the table, he stood.

Michelle could see where he'd gone from where she was sitting, but I couldn't. I turned to look. I saw him reach the bar and take his place next to a woman who was also waiting to be served. She was leaning on her forearms, and had dropped her head, looking towards where the barmaid was. She was one of the actresses from last week, I realised, catching her profile: younger looking; shorter looking, with tatty blonde hair instead of a heavy plait, but certainly her. What was he going to do? What was he going to tell her? I didn't like to think what might be coming next, all because of a book I'd read.

My father did not turn to look at her when he – evidently – said something aimed at her. He'd startled her, I could see that. She looked confounded by whatever he had said: likely some jab about the play, which, if she didn't 'get' the first time, he'd have just kept repeating at her. Something like, let's say, 'Where're your books?' Now she faced him. She wasn't saying much. She listened to him with a bland expression while reaching one hand across the bar and flickering her fingers for the pink-haired barmaid's attention.

My father pointed over at us, and she turned to look, too. There it was. Now we were in play. I went back to my food: a few last twists of pasta, which I had a mouthful of when he came back with this actress, who could hardly say no to meeting two girls who loved theatre, or loved her (or whatever he'd told her). She had her arms crossed, and had wisely left her bottle of water on the bar, to be returned to.

'I had to stop myself standing up and shouting!' my father was saying as they reached our table, and then he looked at her and smiled proudly, as if he were to be wondered at for his unique sensitivity, for his strength of feeling, and for this feat of self-control: not to have stood up and shouted during a play.

She smiled at Michelle and me. She was ready to be friendly to the children. Then she was ready to leave. She was wearing a floral dress, and trainers and a big bobbly cardigan. Her legs were stocky and glossy.

'Look who I've found!' my father said, to me. Then, 'Don't recognise her?'

'She doesn't recognise you!' he said.

'You saw her last week,' he said. And then, taking hold of my shoulder, 'My daughter's the world's expert on Chekhov.'

'Oh,' the actress said. 'Is that so?' Her accent was different. Irish? (Northern Irish, I read later. Her name was Patricia Sweeney. I found her entry in the programme when I got home.)

I didn't know how to speak to strangers back then. I just shook my head.

'And you do drama, don't you, at school?' he said to Michelle, who said, 'Yeah.'

It seemed Patricia Sweeney should be excited to meet us, rather than the other way around. Which was doubly odd, because nobody was being met, really. No, the whole encounter – this coup – only meant anything because of how it might be brought out of the trophy cabinet later on. He would enjoy telling his sisters and his mother about this.

'It was her first time in a theatre last week,' my father said, giving my shoulder a shake. (This wasn't true.)

'Now we want to see backstage,' he said. 'They'd love to see a dressing room. They're dead keen.'

Again, Patricia Sweeney was taken by surprise.

'Well, a dressing room, I mean, it's quite busy back there when there's a production on! A lot of people working. Did you know the Everyman do tours that you can book? I hear they're great. You learn about the history of the theatre and you can have a go with the costumes and some of the effects and so on.'

Here she smiled at Michelle and me. Lifted her eyebrows. I'm afraid I couldn't respond. My father, meanwhile, was sucking his teeth.

'I only have them very rarely,' he said. 'They're dead keen.'

She looked over at us again.

'OK. Let me go and check. Lee, is it? I may be able to take you through for five minutes. I'll see how it's looking.'

And she was off, stopping to collect her bottle and her glass of ice from the bar and to mouth a thank you to the barmaid.

'Get your coats on,' my father said, and we retrieved our damp ski coats from under the benches while he found his and zipped it up. We didn't wait there for Patricia Sweeney to check what she needed to and come back for us but left our drinks and hurried to follow our father, who was already following her, out of the door she'd just left by, and up the stairs and past the box office, where a door marked PRIVATE swung closed behind her. We all waited by that door. My father stood with his chin up and his eyes narrowed.

A few minutes later she came back and did what he'd wanted. She said, 'Ah. You're here.' And then, 'OK, come on through,' and, 'Mind that cable.'

It was crowded in her dressing room with four of us, and three of us in big padded coats, sticking together by the door. Eventually Michelle moved farther into the room and I followed. There were two chairs, in front of a long mirror with light bulbs around it, just like in films.

'So I share with Marie,' Patricia Sweeney said, 'that is Olga, if you remember?' She said this to me, and I looked back blankly.

She sat down in her chair and pulled off her trainers, revealing little white socks with dirty soles. She unscrewed her water and poured some out. Then she took the lime wedge and squeezed it.

There was a full Marks & Spencer shopping bag on the other chair. I could see a bag of posh crisps, and a bunch of black grapes in glinting cellophane. And hummus, which was what we'd just had downstairs, I realised, pleased to put the two together.

I didn't say anything and nor did Michelle.

'As you can see, there's a lot of hairpins involved,' Patricia Sweeney said, talking to me in the mirror. There was a Tupperware box full of them in front of her, which she shook and rattled with her free hand, before stroking her fingers through the mixture.

'And there, if you turn around . . .'

I turned and found a rail of blouses and long skirts, and a black dress on a mannequin. On a shelf were two dented polystyrene heads wearing wigs.

Our father didn't say anything either. Didn't ask any questions. There was nothing he wanted to know. He was standing very still as she explained the tannoy system to Michelle and me and told us that the noises we could hear outside – coordinating shouts and trundles – were the stage being 'reset'. Finally she got Michelle to pass her a cigarette from her coat pocket. Hers was a heavy brown herringbone overcoat, hanging on the back wall. Patricia Sweeney caught my father's eye in the mirror as she lit her cigarette, before smiling blandly again.

'So. That's that. Can you find your way back, Lee, or will I walk you?'

'Find our way, yeah,' he said, and he stretched out his jaw and walked out.

By the following week he was boasting about his 'private tour'.

Soon enough 'My mate Pat' was enlisted in his retinue.

Two or three years later, his interest flared again, when she started to appear on television.

'Did you see my mate Pat's shown up in *EastEnders* now?' he said one week.

'Playing an old boot!'

'Days of the Chekhov classics long behind *her* then!' he said.

But I was nearly sixteen. The end was in sight. I paid him almost no heed at all. ∎

CONTRIBUTORS

Jason Allen-Paisant is a Jamaican poet whose first collection, *Thinking with Trees*, will be published by Carcanet Press in 2021. His work has also appeared in *PN Review*, the *Poetry Review* and *Callaloo*. He teaches in the School of English at the University of Leeds.

Eva Baltasar has published ten volumes of poetry to widespread acclaim. Her debut novel, *Permafrost*, received the 2018 Premi Llibreter from Catalan booksellers and was shortlisted for France's 2020 Prix Médicis for Best Foreign Novel. The author lives with her wife and two daughters in a village near the mountains.

Paul Dalla Rosa is a writer based in Melbourne, Australia. His stories have appeared in *Granta*, *McSweeney's*, *Meanjin* and *New York Tyrant*.

Jesse Darling is an artist based in London and Berlin. Their work has been exhibited at Tate Britain and the Venice Biennale, among other places.

Nate Duke's work has been published in the *Colorado Review*, *Southern Humanities Review*, the *Arkansas International* and elsewhere. He is a PhD candidate in creative writing at Florida State University.

Rory Gleeson is a novelist, playwright and screenwriter. His debut novel, *Rockadoon Shore*, was published by John Murray in 2017.

His short film, *Psychic*, premiered at the Galway Film Fleadh in 2018 and his 2019 play *Blood in the Dirt* debuted at the New Theatre in Dublin. He was a 2019 Burgess Fellow at the University of Manchester, and was awarded a literature bursary in 2020 by Arts Council Ireland.

Duane Hall is a member of the Confederated Tribes of the Colville Reservation.

Lindsey Hilsum is the International Editor of *Channel 4 News*. Her most recent book, *In Extremis: The Life of War Correspondent Marie Colvin* won the James Tait Black Prize for Biography. This is her third essay on Rwanda for *Granta*. 'Where is Kigali?' was published in *Granta* 51: Big Men (and LA Women), and 'The Rainy Season' was published in *Granta* 125: After the War.

Ian Jack edited *Granta* between 1995 and 2007. He is working, not very quickly, on a book about the River Clyde.

Diaa Jubaili was born in Basra, Iraq, where he still lives. He is the author of eight novels and three short-story collections, including *No Windmills in Basra*, winner of the 2018 Almultaqa Prize for the Arabic Short Story, and *What Will We Do Without Calvino?*, winner of the Tayeb Salih International Award for Creative Writing. He was a contributor to the science-fiction anthology *Iraq +100* and has written for the *Guardian*.

Gus Palmer is a documentary photographer and film-maker based in London. He has contributed to Channel 4, Al Jazeera, the *British Journal of Photography* and the *Washington Post*. He was one of the producers on the BBC's *Once Upon a Time in Iraq* and is currently working on a BBC series about the global response to Covid-19.

Vidyan Ravinthiran is the author of two books of poetry: *Grun-tu-molani* and *The Million-Petalled Flower of Being Here*, a Poetry Book Society Recommendation that was shortlisted for both the T.S. Eliot Prize and the Forward Prize. He has also written an award-winning book on Elizabeth Bishop. He teaches at Harvard University.

Gwendoline Riley is the author of five novels: *Cold Water, Sick Notes, Joshua Spassky, Opposed Positions* and *First Love*. 'My Phantoms' is an extract from a forthcoming novel of the same title, published by Granta Books in April 2021. *First Love* was awarded the Geoffrey Faber Memorial Prize.

Chip Rossetti is an Arabic–English translator and book publisher. His published translations include Sonallah Ibrahim's *Beirut, Beirut*, Ahmed Khaled Towfik's *Utopia* and Magdy El Shafee's *Metro: A Story of Cairo*. His translations have appeared in the *White Review*,

Asymptote, Banipal and *Words Without Borders*.

Julia Sanches translates from Portuguese, Spanish and Catalan. Her translations include: from the Portuguese, *Now and at the Hour of Our Death* by Susana Moreira Marques; from the Catalan, *Permafrost* by Eva Baltasar; and from the Spanish, *Slash and Burn* by Claudia Hernández, for which she won a PEN/Heim grant.

Poppy Sebag-Montefiore is a writer and broadcast journalist. Her essay 'Touch', for *Granta* 146: The Politics of Feeling, won a 2021 Pushcart Prize, and has been translated into Chinese for the Beijing-based literary magazine *Dan Du*. She is currently at work on a novel.

Dan Shurley is the author of the chapbook *Collective Regeneration and Universal Love* (Nomadic Press). His reviews and essays have appeared in *BOMB, Asymptote, 3:AM Magazine* and elsewhere. He currently teaches at Immaculata University and lives in Philadelphia.

Fergus Thomas is a British photographer. He specialises in long-term photographic projects, and undertakes assignments and commissions. He has worked for the *Telegraph Magazine*, the *Wall Street Journal* and Four Paws International.

Not yet a subscriber?

Since 1979, *Granta* has provided a platform for the best new writing. These pages defined the literary genre Dirty Realism, tracked down a deposed South American dictator, documented the fall of Saigon, invented the Best of Young Novelists format, published twenty-seven Nobel laureates and highlighted the literary landscapes of Brazil, Canada, India, Ireland, Japan, Pakistan and Spain.

Don't miss out.

Subscribe now from £34/$42 per year.
Digital subscriptions also available from £12/$16.

Visit granta.com/subscribe for details.

GRANTA